THE LAST CHRISTMAS

BY

THOMAS ALEXANDER

The Last Christmas by Thomas Alexander

Direct Light Publications
45 Dudley Court, Endell Street, London, WC2H 9RF

Permissions may be sought directly from NY Publishing Rights Department
45 Dudley Court, Endell Street, London, WC2H 9RF
Library of Congress Cataloguing in Publication Data
Application submitted.
British Library Cataloguing in Publication Data
Application submitted.
04 05 06 07 08 10 9 8 7 6 5 4 3 2

–

Edited by Shirin Laghai for Direct Light Publications.

Cover design by SimplyA

SYNOPSIS

BRUCE Fuck you! In three months' time I'll be back on the nine and you'll be back doing infomercials for PBS. Excuse me if I don't want you to take me with you because you think you have a higher sense of journalistic value that me!

SARAH I do have a higher sense of journalistic value than you! And you know what? All your Taliban bullshit. I don't believe a fucking word of it! You're not doing this because you think it's not news, you're doing this because I got you bumped to the morning!

Set in real time with a script that allows for the incorporation of up to the minute news stories from the time of production, The Last Christmas is a newsroom drama in the Hollywood tradition, exposing the corporate underbelly of national news in a furious, fast-paced moral comedy/drama where the clock is always ticking.

When a leading young producer on a national network runs a story her network disagrees with she finds herself bumped to the graveyard shift along with her on-air anchor.

Forced to work Christmas morning amidst a skeleton staff of misfits, Sarah once more finds herself up against the network when the story of the millennium falls into her lap. With less than an hour until air, Sarah finds her sense of morality pushed to its limit as she battles to put on a story that nobody wants to hear and everybody refuses to tell. A story which could ruin Christmas once and for all.

ABOUT THE AUTHOR

Thomas Alexander has worked in almost all forms of theatre, from opera to children's performances, working as everything from stage hand to costume designer, and has seen his work translated into four different languages and performed as far afield as America and Afghanistan.

His complete plays, along with his first novel, *A Scattering Of Orphans,* have been published by Direct Light Publications.

Also by the Author

PLAYS

Happiness
Murder Me Gently
The Family
Begat
The Crossroads Country
Great
The Visitor
When Dusk Brings Glory
The Recruitment Officer
Writer's Block
The Last Christmas
Writing William
The Big Match

ONE ACT PLAYS

Four Widows and A Funeral
For Arts Sake
The TV
Life TM
The Dance

ADAPTATIONS

William Shakespeare's' R3
Othello

NOVELS

A Scattering Of Orphans
The Disengenuous Martyr

FOREWORD

There is an approach in the news business called the three crop photo, where a picture is cropped in three different ways to tell three different stories.

The first picture shows a soldier handing a bottle of water to a bedraggled man on the side of a road, billows of smoke behind them talking to the ravages of war against the face of humanity, the man's arms reaching out for the bottle in gratitude. The second photo shows another soldier possibly about to shoot, his gun pointed at the same unarmed man sitting on the side of the road, reaching out in front of him as if pleading to God for his life.

The third picture is the complete frame. Pulled back. The man is a prisoner. One soldier is pointing his gun at him, preventing his escape, while the other distributes bottles of water. Three shots from the same photo. Three different stories.

This Rashomon effect is everything that is wrong, not with the news media, but with how we demand our news. I have often wondered at the success in the Royal Court or National Theatre of plays that show the brutality of life, the underbelly of modern society. Set in places like Stockport or Bradford, these plays depict life on housing estates or broken homes. Dark plays that tell of hopelessness and degradation. These plays do amazingly well in the Capital but rarely so well on the road, where plays that you can tap along to prosper and entertain.

The disparity is often put down to education, but there is something more insidious to be found in the box office receipts. There is something almost self-congratulatory about watching the denizens of the National Theatre pouring out onto the South Bank having just watched two hours of squalor on a housing estate. Something shallow and fickle. Something arrogant and vain.

"We have learnt," it seems to say. "We are educated! And isn't it a shame that the people who clean our streets, collect our rubbish, build our products, or are forced out of work by the factories we own closing in disused communities have to live this way!"

I am not a class warrior and there is nothing in the following play that speaks toward this disparity, but it does speak to our penchant for news. We want to be educated, we want to know what is going on in the world, but we want it to fit within the narratives of our life. Phrases like 'cold open', 'bottom ten', 'below the break', and the like; these are natural human reactions when faced with the enormity of the world around us. We need to break it down. We need it bite-sized. We need meat with our veg.

In today's world of wiretaps, paparazzi, and fear-factor, there is an almost resigned enmity to the role of corporations in news media. They are everything that is wrong with the news, we cry. Profits and special interest groups have perverted the media beyond recognition! This is not the news that we want! Forgetting all the while that we are the ones who increasingly use outlets like Facebook to tell us what news we should care about and click on links that take us to houses that look like Hitler, while changing the channel on the banality of human suffering.

We want our news to fit within the narrative of our lives. Forgive the media outlets for giving us exactly what we want.

Thomas Alexander – 2014

The Last Christmas was first produced for New Worlds Theatre Company in Nakameguro, Tokyo, Janurary 2008, at Woody Theatre.

ORIGINAL CAST

SARAH	Rachel Walzer
DAVID	Antun Percec
BRUCE	Michael Mitchell
AL	Patrick Smith
CHRIS	Sophie Cartman
CHAD	Dejan Skaljac
JOSIE	Emilie Adams
ALAN	Mark Sommers
DARREN	Andrew Woolner
MAKE UP GIRL	Maiko Oshida

...and featuring the voices of Chris Parham, Martin Burns, and Alec Harris.

Directed and Produced by Alec Harris.

Stage Manager	Francis Sommerville
Assistant Director	Claudia Hamann
Lighting Design	Jonathan Hagans
Set Construction	Dave Waddington

Special Thanks to The Jewish Community Centre Tokyo, Yokohama Theatre Group, Yasuhiro Fuji, Toriya Walzer, Ann Jenkins, Jack Merluzzi, and various insulted deities.

CAST

SARAH	30s. Strong. Intellectual. Liberal.
DAVID	60s. News Anchor. Charming.
BRUCE	30s. Handsome. Charming. News Anchor.
AL	30s. Arrogant. Funny. Scruffy.
CHRIS	Male/Female. Intense. Quiet. Nice.
CHAD	Early 20s. Non Caucasian. Cocky.
JOSIE	Mid 20s. Pretty.
ALAN	70s. Studio Owner. Commanding. Large.
NADINE	Female. Young.
MAKE UP GIRL	
GARETH	Male. OFF.
TREVOR	V/O
PRIEST	V/O

AUTHORS NOTE

The Last Christmas is set in real time and is designed to run for 90 minutes precisely, starting one hour *before* the start of the news broadcast at the crux of the play. However, it is up to each individual production to decide whether or not they intend to keep this format.

The news stories contained here reflect news current 12/25/2007. It is advisable to update the stories to comparable ones from the closest Christmas. All rights regarding alteration and copyright are waved with respect to marked passages (*>>italicized<<*). However, all other passages remain the copyright of Thomas Alexander. Any and all publication and/or performance by consent only.

(OFF)	Offstage.
(EAR)	Spoken OFF on an inner ear microphone. Purportedly only heard by the actor being directly addressed.
(TANNOY)	Spoken OFF on a loudspeaker system. Heard by all actors on stage.
(V/O)	Voiceover. Can be pre-recorded.

ACT 1

ACT I

LIGHTS UP.

A NEWSROOM – CHRISTMAS DAY.

THE STAGE IS DIVIDED INTO TWO SECTIONS. STAGE RIGHT THE MAIN BODY IS TAKEN UP BY THE CONFERENCE ROOM. A LARGE ROOM WITH A CONFERENCE TABLE SURROUNDED UNTIDILY WITH CHAIRS. A SINGLE DOOR, STAGE RIGHT, LEADS IN.

AT THE FAR END OF THE CONFERENCE ROOM STANDS A LARGE TV SCREEN. ON THE CONFERENCE TABLE, AMIDST A PILE OF RUBBISH, COMPRISING OF OLD COKE CANS AND PAPER CUPS, IS A SPEAKER-PHONE. A COAT RACK IS NEAR THE DOOR.

STAGE LEFT IS A SMALLER ROOM: SARAH'S OFFICE. THE OFFICE IS SET FACING THE CONFERENCE ROOM. A LARGE OAK BUSINESS DESK WITH A FEW SEATS DOTTED AROUND THE ROOM IS ALL THERE IS. A LAPTOP COMPUTER, TURNED OFF, SITS ON AN OTHERWISE SPARTAN DESK, A SHARP CONTRAST TO THE CONFERENCE ROOM.

SARAH ENTERS, BALANCING A PILE OF PAPERS AND A WARM WINTER COAT ALONG WITH A STYROFOAM CUP OF COFFEE, GRIPPED BY HER TEETH.

SHE MAKES IT TO THE TABLE BUT SPILLS THE PAPERS AS SHE TRIES TO PUT THEM DOWN ON THE TABLE. THEY GET LOST IN THE SURROUNDING MESS. GRABBING A PIECE AT RANDOM SHE MOVES ACROSS THE ROOM, DEPOSITING HER COAT ON THE RACK AS SHE READS, BEFORE HEADING BACK TO THE TABLE AND MOVING, COFFEE IN HAND, TO THE HEAD OF THE TABLE, STILL READING.

SHE SITS. STILL READING SHE PULLS OUT HER MOBILE PHONE AND DIALS A NUMBER. SHE GETS NOWHERE WITH IT AND HITS ANOTHER NUMBER. NOW INTENT ON THE PHONE SHE SCROLLS AND HITS ANOTHER NUMBER, TO NO AVAIL. PUSHING PAPERS ASIDE, SHE PICKS UP THE

PHONE ON THE DESK AND HITS A NUMBER.

SARAH   (INTO THE PHONE) Good. You're in. (BEAT) No, not yet. Listen; who's open on Christmas Day? (PAUSE) No, shops. (BEAT) Now, yeah. (PAUSE) There's not, a Seven-Eleven or something… (PAUSE) No. Fine. Just, forgot something, that's all. (PAUSE) Yeah, I'll send them down as soon as they get in. (SHE GOES TO HANG UP THEN CATCHES HERSELF) Right, yeah, Merry Christmas.

CHAD ENTERS AS THOUGH PASSING THE DOOR AND SEEING SARAH INSIDE. UNSEEN BY SARAH, HE HESITATES, LOOKING AT HIS WATCH, THEN RAPS ON THE DOOR.

CHAD   Hi.

SARAH   Can I help you?

CHAD   (ENTERING AND OFFERING A HAND) Ms. Ziegler?

SARAH   (IGNORING THE HAND INSTINCTIVELY) Sarah. Do I…

CHAD   Sarah. Right.

SARAH   Can I… I'm sorry, I didn't get your name?

CHAD   Chad. C. Whatever, it's fine.

SARAH   How did you… Really? Chad

CHAD   My parents were big Gunsmoke fans.

SARAH   There was a Chad on Gunsmoke?

CHAD   (SHRUGGING) They were all called Chad.

SARAH   I see. (BEAT) Chad, you mind me asking how you got back here?

CHAD   There was no one at the desk and…

SARAH   Yeah, well, look, you know, it's good to take an interest but; well, (POINTING TO AN EMPTY CORNER OF THE ROOM) you see that camera up there?

CHAD   (LOOKING) Actually..?

SARAH   Yeah well, like I said, it's flattering and everything but it takes about, you know, three minutes for security to get down here and, well, the whole 'Chad' thing took a minute, if you know what I mean.

CHAD   Actually…

SARAH   (GETTING UP) Like I said, it's good to see people taking an interest in how the news is made and everything but this is a secure set and…

CHAD   I wasn't….

SARAH   If you want some tickets, I'm sure the guy at the desk can hook you up with, you know, the Daily Show or something but see, this is a news show, we don't use an audience and…

CHAD   I'm sorry. Look. There, um, there seems to be a misunderstanding. I work here!

SARAH   (TRYING TO USHER HIM OUT) Yeah, sure, nice one.

CHAD   Seriously.

SARAH   Seriously. Security. Thirty seconds.

CHAD   I'm the new intern!

SARAH   (STOPPING) Come again?

CHAD   Intern. Uncle Alan…

SARAH   Wait. You're Alan Smith's nephew?

CHAD   I just…

SARAH   You're Alan Smith's little nephew from Phoenix?

CHAD   I'm adopted.

SARAH   You're really Alan Smith's nephew?

CHAD   C. Smith. Chad.

SARAH   Chad, eh. (GOING BACK TO THE DESK) Well, Merry Christmas me.

CHAD   Look, I want you to know that, I know, it's… (HE STARTS AGAIN) Using your uncle's name to, you know, get a position and everything is hardly…

SARAH   What are you doing here, Chad?

CHAD   You know. I wanna learn.

SARAH   No, I mean; what are you doing here! The email said… It's Christmas Day. Shouldn't you be at your uncle's, opening (BEAT) a sport channel or something?

CHAD   I thought…

SARAH   (TURNING HER BACK ON HIM) Yeah, you know, I don't have time for this. It's Christmas, Chad. I've got a news show in exactly (LOOKS AT THE CLOCK) less time than I need and I don't have the cold open. Come back after the holidays, okay?

CHAD   Tampa.

SARAH   I'm sorry?

CHAD   Tampa. Two years. You were a runner, got some print on, moved into the production booth. Then Michigan. More running, three years, bigger strides. Nothing in print, nothing on the air. Then the company got picked up by Newscorp. Suddenly they like your copy. Six months at the U.N. Eight months behind the desk; two a.m., graveyard shift. Then it's New York, eleven p.m. CNN, eight a.m. CNBC, morning with Cathy, backstep I guess, but they bump you to the six as assistant, then producer and you run it for five years before we bring you in here.

SARAH   We.

CHAD   Sorry?

SARAH   You said we; "we brought you in here."

CHAD   (EMBARRASSED) I'm sorry, that just came out. I didn't…

SARAH   Don't worry about it. (BEAT) All right, Chad, if that is your name, that little lesson in stalker bravado earned you a week.

CHAD   Thank you. You won't…

SARAH   What are we paying you?

CHAD   You're not.

SARAH   (PULLING MONEY OUT OF HER POCKET) Good. There's a coffee place on the corner. Six double lattes with two shots in each but, (BEAT) and here's the thing Chad, here's what separates the wheat from the chaff, the interns from the Chads, you ready?

CHAD   Shoot.

SARAH   Don't tempt me. Six double lattes, with two shots in each, but the cups? I want them to read soy decaf, got it?

CHAD   Decaf?

SARAH   You got it.

CHAD   On the cups?

SARAH   Exactly.

CHAD   Can I ask why?

SARAH   First lesson in the news business. Vanity is everything. Staying awake is more.

CHAD   What if they're not open?

SARAH   Wheat from the Chads!

CHAD   Got it. (HE TURNS TO GO AND THEN STOPS AT THE DOOR) This is some kind of test to see if I'm going to push my weight around, isn't it?

SARAH   Honestly, Chad? It's just a way to get you to leave.

ENTER DAVID.

CHAD   (EXITING) Hi.

DAVID   Hi.

EXIT CHAD.

SARAH TURNS BACK TO THE TABLE, READING.

DAVID   Hey.

SARAH   Hey.

DAVID   Merry Christmas.

SARAH   Did you see this?

DAVID   Who's the kid? See what?

SARAH   They're saying people in India, well, men anyway, they're saying the reason birth control isn't working is that normal sized condoms are too large.

DAVID   Too large?

SARAH   Apparently they're coming up with 'Indian sized'. I mean, way to destroy the self confidence of an entire sub-continent. Imagine waking up one morning and finding that you're batting with a piccolo, globally speaking.

DAVID   Can we even report that?

SARAH   And who in their right mind is gonna to buy 'Indian' condoms now? It's gonna be like; "five packs of American super size and, what the hell, throw in an Indian, while you're at it. I'm training the little one to make balloon animals."

DAVID   Can we even say 'condoms'?

SARAH   Well not twenty times real fast, no.

DAVID   You know what I mean.

SARAH   I do. And I don't know. FCC being what it is.

DAVID   Something for the nine then. Who's the kid in the
corridor?

SARAH   Intern. Don't ask.

DAVID   You know, I wished you a Merry Christmas.

SARAH   Yeah?

DAVID   Some parts of the world that might be considered
repetitious.

SARAH   I didn't hear you.

DAVID   Some parts of the world a wife might even kiss her
husband hello.

SARAH   (PICKING UP OTHER PAPERS) I kissed you.

DAVID   That was in the bed.

SARAH   Where kissing is meant for. My mother raised me
properly.

DAVID   Your mother raised you on a commune in Waco.
(POINTING TO A PAPER ON THE DESK) That the overnights?

SARAH   (PICKING THE PAPER UP) Yeah. Listen; you seen Al anywhere, his car's in the lot…

DAVID   Not since yesterday. Why?

SARAH   His car was in the lot.

DAVID   Anything in the overnights?

SARAH   Bombing in Kinshasa, that cult thing just got started in Malaysia…

DAVID   Guess they don't have Christmas there either.

SARAH   …more talk on the shooting, but actually no.

DAVID   I meant the overnights.

SARAH   Five point two, seven percent share. Don't worry about it.

DAVID   (DEFLATED) Right.

SARAH   Don't worry about it. It was Christmas Eve.

DAVID   It was a big story.

SARAH   Don't worry about it.

DAVID   We didn't ramp it properly.

SARAH   It was Christmas Eve!

DAVID   A ten second spot on the nine was never going to be enough.

SARAH   I'm saying it was Christmas Eve. Unless you were doing a live sexcapade with Santa it was never going to get more than a six.

DAVID   In my heyday, maybe. Nowadays I don't even rank a three.

SARAH   Don't sell yourself short.

DAVID   It was a good story.

SARAH   I know it was a good story. I was the one who proposed it, remember?

DAVID   I mean an important story.

SARAH   Don't worry about it.

DAVID   To us.

SARAH   (PAUSE) You saying I killed it?

DAVID   I'm saying you could have ramped it a little more. Pushed the division.

SARAH   We got what we got.

DAVID   But not what we needed.

SARAH   You saying this as a husband or as an employee?

DAVID   Both. We needed that. The Albanian thing…

SARAH   (SUDDENLY ANGRY) Jesus, David. It was Christmas Eve! Even Fox didn't rate a goddamned six! It was never going to do what you wanted.

DAVID   It had legs.

SARAH   So does a Christmas tree.

DAVID   Meaning?

SARAH   Meaning you can't keep looking for a goddamned miracle, and you can't keep blaming me for it. It was Christmas Eve! No one wants to hear about corruption at Christmas. Not even Dickens!

DAVID   Yeah.

SARAH   Anyway. It's not like it's your job.

DAVID   (PAUSE) About that.

SARAH   Really? (BEAT) No. Later.

DAVID   Listen…

SARAH   (WARNING) No!

DAVID   We have to talk about it sometime.

SARAH   Bruce, right? I don't want to talk about it.

DAVID   You have to talk about it sometime.

SARAH   All right. Tell me. (BEAT) No! I don't want to know.

DAVID   Sarah…

SARAH   It's wrong!

DAVID   It's not!

SARAH   Really?

DAVID   Okay, it's wrong, but it's where we are.

SARAH   It's Christmas.

DAVID   What's that got to do with it?

SARAH   Good will to all men and all that shit.

DAVID   You have to talk about it sometime.

SARAH   Well I'm not talking about it today, alright.

DAVID   Tomorrow might be too late.

SARAH   No one gets fired at Christmas, David. Even network executives saw A Christmas Carol when they were kids.

DAVID   The Muppet version maybe.

SARAH   Not today, alright. And not in this office! Where the hell is everyone?

DAVID   "Light the lamp, not the rat. Light the lamp, not the rat."

SARAH   It's amazing to me that I ever found you attractive.

DAVID   Speaking of which. Did you see that thing with the girl?

SARAH   The actress?

DAVID   It was on the radio on the way in.

SARAH   What have I told you about listening to radio news?

DAVID   She must have made her parents proud.

SARAH   It's not news.

DAVID   Yeah.

SARAH   It's barely even entertainment.

AL WAKES UP.

THERE'S A LOUD BUMP FROM UNDER THE TABLE. AL SITS UP, BASHING HIS HEAD ON THE TABLE AND YELLS IN PAIN.

| SARAH | Jesus! |

AL   Ow.

DAVID   Al?

SARAH   Jesus!

AL   Just Al.

SARAH   Jes... Al?! What...

DAVID   My god, you look like crap.

AL STRUGGLES INTO A CHAIR.

SARAH   It's the smell I was thinking about.

AL   Thought everyone went home.

DAVID   It's 7:30 Al! Christmas?

SARAH   You've been here all night?

AL   There's a morning?

SARAH   And look what Santa brought you, (SHOUTING)
a hangover!

AL   I think I'm gonna puke.

DAVID   (POINTING AT THE DOOR)You want me to..?

SARAH   Please. (DAVID GOES TO EXIT) And while you're
there can you check Sally's still alive in make up? She didn't sound so
good earlier and I think we're going to be cutting it tight.

DAVID   No problem.

EXIT DAVID.

AL   I'm just gonna rest my eyes for a bit, alright?

SARAH   (SWEETLY) No problem.

SHE WAITS A SECOND WHILE AL STARTS TO DOZE OFF,
THEN RAISES THE PAPERS AND BANGS THEM DOWN ON
THE DESK, STARTLING AL.

AL   I'm awake!

SARAH   You slept on the floor!?

AL   Wait. (BEAT) Yes. Yes. There was a girl...

11

SARAH   You're the head writer for a national news show Al.
You don't just sleep on the floor!

DAVID RETURNS WITH TWO CUPS OF COFFEE.

AL   What time is it?

DAVID   Seven thirty-five.

AL   Three questions then. Was there a war?

DAVID   Which one?

AL   A new one. With us.

DAVID   No.

SARAH   Jesus!

AL   Taylor Swift still alive?

DAVID   Unfortunately, yes.

AL   Jesus return?

DAVID   There's time. Drink the coffee.

AL   (RETURNING TO SLEEP) Wake me at 8:30
then.

ENTER JOSIE.

SARAH   The coffee can either go down your throat or down
your pants. It's totally up to you.

AL   I am totally awake.

JOSIE   David, Sarah.

AL   Ow.

SARAH   Where the hell is everyone?

JOSIE   I saw Bruce at the elevator.

SARAH   How was make up? (TO JOSIE) What do you mean
you saw him in the elevator?

DAVID   Strangely fine. Didn't get a Merry Christmas out of
her either.

JOSIE   I mean, I saw him in the elevator!

SARAH   So? What? He just kept going up?

JOSIE   I think he went to his office.

SARAH   His office! Jesus. David, could you go see if Bruce
wants to…

ENTER BRUCE.

SARAH   (CONT.) Finally!

JOSIE   Sarah, can I talk to you for a minute?

BRUCE   Morning all. Sorry I'm late.

SARAH   It's gonna have to wait, Josie. Have a seat.

BRUCE   I'd blame the traffic but… well.

SARAH   So long as you're here. Alright. Everyone, have a
seat! We're gonna have to get through this quickly.

BRUCE   Where's Chris?

SARAH   We'll get through the overnights then…

BRUCE   I don't think there's much point starting until Chris
gets here.

SARAH   We'll… It's nearly eight…

AL   That went quick.

SARAH   …so I think we'll have to get going without her.

BRUCE   I'm not starting without Chris.

THE ROOM GOES SILENT.

SARAH   I'm sorry?

BRUCE   She's the control room manager!

SARAH   And I'm the producer. Take a seat and let's get
started.

DAVID   We've got the overnights.

BRUCE   (SITTING) I didn't mean…

SARAH   Alright everyone. Listen up. (LOOKING AT AL)
Al!

AL   Present.

DAVID   Not until after dinner.

SARAH   You've all done this before. Most is in the can but it's a skeleton staff today, seeing as it's the holidays, so let's just get through this and we can all get off to our loved ones.

AL   I thought you loved one here.

SARAH   I want to run through the overnights, see if there's anything we want to push or bump…

AL   See what I did there?

SARAH   …then we'll go round the table.

AL   Dangling modifier joke while hungover.

DAVID   I think you're the joke and the modifier's over hung.

AL   Touché.

SARAH   Alright, first…

BRUCE   Touchy.

SARAH   Kinshasa.

AL   Done to death. Literally.

SARAH   Car bomb. Three dead.

BRUCE   I'm with Al. It's nothing new. It was the lead a year ago but now…

SARAH   Heaven forbid we should care.

AL   It's old.

SARAH   Alright, but we've got to report it.

DAVID   Do we have graphics?

SARAH   I looked at the tape on the way in. Nothing spectacular. Same ten seconds as everyone else.

BRUCE   End the ten with it. Shows we care, says it's not new.

AL   I agree.

SARAH   And sadly, so do I. Alright. Let's make it… We'll have to push the Japanese ice dipping. Doesn't go too well.

DAVID   That's the lead in the twenty?

AL   What have we got in the twenty?

SARAH   Bethlehem. Santa's arrest. Justin Beiber and the
>>*WGA*<<.

AL   Santa then.

DAVID   You can make that? Car bomb to homeless Santa?

AL   (POINTING TO HIMSELF) Writer!

SARAH   Al?

AL   Pathos. Feel bad, poor Santa, yadda yadda yadda.

SARAH   Alright, switch Santa and… any room in the twenty
for Indian condoms?

AL   (SERIOUS) Not without graphics.

SARAH   Alright. I'll pass it to the nine team then.

AL   Feel I missed a good joke there.

DAVID   We did it.

AL   Where was I?

DAVID   Under the table.

BRUCE   I take it we're doing something on the actress.

DAVID/SARAH No.

AL   What actress.

JOSIE   It was on the radio.

DAVID   Some actress…

BRUCE   Some actress decided she wouldn't wear… I'm
sorry, she wouldn't wear, you know, underwear to a party, got drunk
and fell over outside the nightclub. CNN's running pictures.

SARAH   And what have I told you about watching CNN!

AL   Which actress?

DAVID   The slutty one.

AL   They're all slutty.

JOSIE   The one in the movie about the… thing.

AL   That's why we love 'em.

SARAH   It's not news.

AL   We got footage?

DAVID SWINGS HIS LAPTOP AROUND AND HANDS IT TO AL.

SARAH   Can we..!

DAVID   It's all over the internet.

AL LOOKS AT A PICTURE.

AL   Wow. Brazilian. Bold choice!

SARAH   It's not news and we're not running it.

BRUCE   Six million households might disagree.

AL   And three billion men.

DAVID   It's out there already.

SARAH   It is. And it's Christmas and if little Johnny is going to look at some inebriated girl's privates while he opens his presents, it's not going to be on this network.

BRUCE   Yeah, but…

SARAH   Bruce. Seriously. It's a slow news day. Let's just get through this and go home, alright?

AL   Hang on.

SARAH   Seriously…

AL   Hang on. (TO SARAH) You see this?

SARAH   Al…

AL   There's… a five year old girl in Delhi was…

BRUCE   This was last month?

JOSIE   What girl?

AL   Last month, this month… You think India gives a shit about…

DAVID   Some girl, a kid really; baby was abducted from her home…

AL   They're saying the police did nothing about it.

DAVID	She was tortured and raped. Five years old.
AL	(TO SARAH) You saw this?
SARAH	Reuters, yeah.
JOSIE	When was this?
DAVID	Last night.
SARAH	There's nothing on it in the dailies so…
AL	How… what is this? A national sport or something?
DAVID	Well, the BBC…
AL	Why are we not doing a piece now?
SARAH	And say what?

AL   That it happened! That this is a country who are so closed minded that even talking about a crime to the media gets you a double sentence. And if just let it go at that…

SARAH   And say what? That it happened? You know how many women were raped in the US last night that we're not reporting!

AL   This is corruption! The police… This is systematic…

SARAH   Alright. Give me thirty seconds of copy and we'll see where we are.

AL   You're not outraged by this?

SARAH   I am! Of course I am! This is a country that's had equal rights for fifty years but can't seem..! This isn't even about religion it's just… they hate women! What do you want from me? (BEAT) Give me thirty seconds, and just the facts, alright? No liberal left-wing shit, got it?

AL   I'm Republican! You're supposed to be the ones burning your bras. This isn't left-wing bias. This is morality one oh one. And if we don't report it now, I don't know who the hell we are!

SARAH   You done?

AL   I'm serious.

SARAH   Then give me in thirty seconds without the whole Patton thing and we will, alright?

DAVID   That's one way to cure a hangover.

SARAH   Alright. Listen up! We got three for the lead. Round the table. Josie? How long was the weather piece?

JOSIE   Three twenty.

BRUCE   Bit long for the lead.

DAVID   I agree.

SARAH   And we're sure about it?

JOSIE   Sure.

SARAH   I mean, we're sure it's not going to snow? You know, like two centimetres somewhere in the country.

JOSIE   It's not.

SARAH   'Cos we'd look a bit stupid saying it's the lowest snowfall on record and then there's a blizzard in Saskatoon.

DAVID   I think that's in Canada.

JOSIE   It's not going to snow.

AL   It is.

JOSIE   Not!

AL   I mean; it is in Canada, but thanks for talking to me.

JOSIE   Go screw yourself!

BRUCE   Are we really going to do this? I mean it's good in the twenty, but in the ten? And the lead?!

SARAH   People want what they want.

BRUCE   I know that, Sarah. I am a professional.

AL   Here we go.

BRUCE   No! I'm a professional, but there's such a thing as news and that's not news!

JOSIE   The weather's not news?

DAVID   If it was right it would be!

SARAH   Let's try to stay with this, shall we? Bruce, I agree with you, but if it stays it stays in the ten. Ski slopes shut, people lose jobs, industries lose money, economies suffer. It's news and it stays in the ten.

DAVID   I've seen the tape. It's good.

SARAH   The two others then. Chicago closed for three hours due to ice…

BRUCE   That the lead!

SARAH   And government funding…

BRUCE   (OVERLAPPING) It's gotta be Chicago!

SARAH   …cu… Hang on!

BRUCE   Al? Human interest. Do a lead with stranded passengers. We've got archive on…

SARAH   Hang on!

DAVID   It's not…

SARAH   Jesus Bruce! Come on! You know how this works!

BRUCE   I'm just trying to…

SARAH   It was a water truck. It spilled on a runway and froze before they could clean. It's news but it's not news.

DAVID   It's comedy.

CHAD ENTERS CARRYING THE COFFEE. HE STARTS HANDING THEM OUT. THE REST LOOK AT HIM, SARAH IGNORES HIM.

SARAH   You want something; it runs through me, alright? That's how this works. David?

DAVID   The cuts are good. Great footage. Real human interest. Charity workers moaning etc. etc., it's an important piece but…

SARAH   What?

CHAD   It's sad.

BRUCE   Exactly!

DAVID   It is. And it's Christmas morning and if we come over all grinchy on the cold lead then people are gonna turn off.

CHAD   (TO THE ROOM) Soy decaf?

SARAH   Alright. What have we got then? New York. Cuts. Chicago. Weather. Kinshasa?

AL   Yep.

DAVID   Sounds right to me.

CHAD   (TO JOSIE) Hi.

JOSIE   Yeah.

SARAH   Alright. Al…

BRUCE   I'm going to makeup.

SARAH   Not yet.

AL   I'm thinking 2.10 for N.Y., 2.40 for cuts, 1.50 for Chicago. 1.30 clean for Kinshasa.

SARAH   What I thought. 8.10. Josie, you're going to need to cut the weather thing, alright, I want you to speak to Chris when she gets in. David, you'll work with her. Keep the economy side of it but cut back on the H.I., we've got enough of that already.

JOSIE   Right. H.I.?

SARAH   Human interest. Work with David and…

AL   I'm sorry, it's maybe because I'm still a little drunk but… who is this and why is he giving me decaf?

SARAH   He's not. Chad. Everyone. Everyone. Chad.

DAVID   Seriously? Chad?

CHAD   I was born there.

SARAH   Chad is our new intern.

DAVID   We had an old one?

SARAH   And he also happens to be Alan Smith's nephew.

CHAD   Thanks.

SARAH   My pleasure.

AL   Hang on. You're…

CHAD   Adopted.

AL   Damn. Angelina Jolie or Alan Smith. Talk about the short end!

SARAH   If we could get back to this…

ENTER CHRIS.

CHRIS HURRIES INTO THE ROOM. EVERYONE LOOKS UP AT HER. IT'S CLEAR SHE'S AGITATED AND BEEN HERE FOR A WHILE.

SARAH   Glad you could… What?

CHRIS   This everyone?

BRUCE   We were discussing the…

DAVID   Chris?

CHRIS   Who's the kid?

DAVID   Better not to ask.

CHRIS   This… ha. I don't…

SARAH   Everything alright?

CHRIS   Hang on.

SARAH   Chris?

CHRIS   You know, I swear to God, those stairs…

EVERYONE STANDS, SHOCKED.

JOSIE   Terrorism?

DAVID   Chris…

AL   What…

CHAD   Cool.

SARAH   Alright. Let's all calm…

CHRIS   (POINTING AT THE DESK) There's… there's a guy on the phone. He's… Well, I think you have to hear this for yourself.

JOSIE   Are we under attack?

CHRIS   Does anyone here remember Gareth Williams? (EVERYONE LOOKS PERPLEXED) Short guy. Serious.

DAVID   British?

CHRIS   That's the guy.

DAVID   Worked with him the first time in Iraq. Guy's a
bulldog.

SARAH   Chris..?

CHRIS   Well, he's on the phone. From Rome. I've been
running through it upstairs for the past few hours. Car wouldn't start,
had to get a taxi. You try getting a taxi downtown at five a.m. on
Christmas Day.

SARAH   (LOOKING AT THE TABLE) He's on the phone?

DAVID   What's he doing in Rome?

CHRIS   Called me at home. Said he didn't trust anyone else
with it.

DAVID   What's he doing in Rome?

CHRIS   Works there. After Iraq…

SARAH   Could someone clear this shit off the table so we
can see the goddamned phone?

JOSIE STARTS TO CLEAR THINGS OFF.

BRUCE   Chris. Has there been an attack?

CHRIS   What? No! You're just going to have to… I can't
really… well.

AL   You know, if this is something, I could do with the
heads up. 'M drunk.

CHRIS   You're gonna have to listen.

AL   I don't…

SARAH   Everybody calm down. Chris. This isn't masterpiece
theatre. I'm not going into a conference call I know nothing about and
we're under time constraints. (BEAT) Is this something for today or..?

CHRIS   It's the lead.

SARAH   (THINKING FOR A SECOND) Alright.

AL   Can you at least…

SARAH   (MOVING TO THE PHONE) Let's just do this, shall we? What line is he on?

CHRIS   Line one.

THEY ALL MOVE BACK TO THE TABLE. CHRIS STANDS OFF IN THE CORNER.

SARAH   (PRESSING A BUTTON ON THE PHONE) Gareth? (THERE'S SILENCE) Gareth? You there? (SHE SHRUGS AT THE ROOM)

CHRIS   Gareth, it's Chris Barnet.

GARETH   (OFF, GUARDED) Who's that with you?

SARAH   Gareth. This is Sarah Ziegler. I'm news director of the seven, the nine o'clock news. Chris tells us you may have a story?

GARETH   (OFF) The Jew?

DAVID   Gareth. This is David Sachs. We worked together at CBS before the split. (THERE IS SILENCE. SARAH HOLDS UP HER HANDS) Gareth?

CHRIS   Gareth. Time is a little against us here, so why...

GARETH   (OFF) Two years ago the Vatican started to, you know, back up all its filing onto digital. I suppose, I don't know. I suppose the Pope or someone got wind of the internet, but anyway, that's what they did. Library cards. Papal decrees. Everything; shipped into digital. I suppose they thought it would last longer, I don't...

SARAH   What's the story Gareth? Not sure what time it is there but the clock is a little against us here.

GARETH   (OFF, IGNORING) Anyway. So they backed it all up. Everything. All the ages. Last I heard they were up to, like, way past the Middle Ages or something. Everything a Pope ever said, everything they ever ordered, backed up onto hard disk.

AL   What's this...

GARETH   (OFF, ANGRY) I'm getting to it! Would you let me get to it? You need this. This is background. I can't...

SARAH   Go on Gareth.

GARETH   (OFF) So there it is, somewhere in the Vatican all backed up in the basement probably. You know. Every edict of the Pope. The Nazis, the Inquisition. There's been talk about it for years of course. Rumours here, innuendo there. Surprising what you find when you start scanning old files. (PAUSE) You there?

SARAH   We're here Gareth. Go on.

GARETH   (OFF) That whole thing with the grave of St. Paul was supposed to have come from there.

BRUCE   Gareth. This is Bruce Baxter here. Tell us what you got.

GARETH   (OFF) Oh, hey Bruce. You on the morning show now?

SARAH   What have you got Gareth?

GARETH   (OFF) Naturally they keep the whole thing off the grid. Very CIA. You know, like that room in Mission Impossible. Very high tech.

SARAH STABS THE MUTE BUTTON ON THE PHONE.

SARAH   This guy for real?

CHAD   È matto

GARETH   (OFF) There's no entry from outside. No connection. No drives.

AL   But?

GARETH   (OFF) Right. But, I guess people don't think priests need a lot of training in the secure sending of emails. So, anyway, long and short of it is… I've got an email here talking about moving the body of Jesus.

THE ROOM FALLS SILENT.

SARAH   Sorry, Gareth. I think we've lost you here.

GARETH   1942, they move it out of Rome. 1453, they move it overseas…

SARAH   (LOOKING AT CHRIS) Yeah, okay Gareth. Listen. I think it's good. There's a lot of, you know, Da Vinci code people who…

GARETH   (OFF) No, I've got it. Really. Right here. One of the priests, doing the scanning or whatever it is, and I guess he's got a pang of conscience because he's, you know, worried about defrauding the public for the last two thousand years.

AL   (INCREDULOUS) He knows where Jesus was buried?

GARETH   (OFF) Long and short of it. Yes.

SARAH   Hang on Gareth. Let me just get this straight. You're saying that you have an email from a priest to his archbishop saying he knows where Jesus is buried?

CHRIS   He's got it.

SARAH   Yeah, well. Gareth, this is all very interesting but, seriously, the twenty's filled.

CHRIS   No. He's GOT it.

SARAH   Chris, Gareth, I'm sorry. But an email from a raving priest does not a story make.

GARETH   (OFF) Yeah. Cos I've only been a journalist for twenty-eight years. I've got a five centuries old letter from Pope Alexander worried about whether they should move the grave. I've got a signed edict from what's-his-name, allowing the movement of documents to America at the outbreak of World War II. And I've got taped conversations with three priests who'd rather not go on the record with the whole thing if you know what I mean.

AGAIN THE ROOM IS SILENT.

GARETH   (OFF, CONT.) See, I've been a journalist for a while, so, when I say I have it. I have it, alright? I went digging. Found the priest. Seems he's not the only one with pang of conscience. Seems word of it's getting out. So he started gathering information. Taking the ones already been scanned. The originals. I've got him holed up in a B&B in Firenze.

DAVID   Jesus.

AL   Dead, apparently.

BRUCE   Just so we understand, here. Jesus' body…

GARETH   (OFF) Is and always has been in a grave, hidden by the Catholic Church.

THERE IS SILENCE.

CHAD   Where?

CHRIS   He's not saying.

GARETH   (OFF) Technically, I work for you guys, but you
don't run this...

SARAH   Gareth. I'm gonna put you on hold.

GARETH   (OFF) All…

HE'S CUT OFF AS SARAH HITS A BUTTON.

SARAH   Alright. Umm. What are we talking about here?

CHAD   Fraud.

BRUCE   Who are you again?

DAVID   No. He's right. Whichever way you look at it.

AL   Fraud. Perpetrated by the world's largest organization
on the world's largest religion.

BRUCE   Come on!

SARAH   Let's…

BRUCE   It's an email! It's what, documents or something? So
what?

SARAH   Let's go round the table. Chris? You trust this guy?

CHRIS   With this? Yeah. Yeah, I do. Man's got two Peabodys.

SARAH   Shit, I've got a Peabody!

CHRIS   Remember that thing in Iraq? Five guys decide to
shoot up a town. Blackwater. This was him. If he says he's got it, he's
got it.

SARAH   Alright. Al?

AL   Three things. One, and I'm saying that this is real
deal, one, we're gonna get sued. Personally, collectively.

DAVID   By who? Catholics?

AL   The right.

DAVID   We are the right!

AL   Not once we do this we're not.

CHAD   He's right.

AL   We're going to get sued for, well, ruining everything.

SARAH   Second?

AL   Second, we don't run this, someone will.

BRUCE   You can't be serious.

AL   There's a priest out there with a bunch of stolen documents and a conscience. We don't run with this, he'll go somewhere else. He's a whistleblower. Also, and I should add, we start not running stories our reporters give us and we're not gonna keep our reporters. You heard him, he's ready to jump as it is.

SARAH   Third?

AL   (SHRUGGING) It's Christmas.

DAVID   So?

SARAH   You think it'll play badly on a Christian holiday.

AL   Badly? No. It'll end it.

JOSIE   What?

DAVID   I'm not with you.

AL   It's Christmas. Virgin birth. God from man. Jesus didn't die! Jesus hopped on a plane and flew off somewhere, raised a family and died happily...

DAVID   He's supposed to have risen again.

AL   He's dead? End of the religion.

BRUCE   Jesus Christ!

AL   Not if he's dead he's not.

BRUCE   You're actually considering this?

SARAH   It's news.

BRUCE   It's Christmas!

JOSIE   I'm not sure I understand this.

SARAH   Gareth?

GARETH   (OFF) You're not running it.

SARAH   Why'd you say that?

GARETH   (OFF) You're a right-wing conservative station that answers to corporate.

SARAH   We're a right-wing conservative station that answers to corporate, Gareth. They still cut your cheques too.

PAUSE.

SARAH   I'm not saying we're not going to run it but we're in the ninth inning, understand what I'm saying? I need you to get me what you've got on the secure server.

CHRIS   We've got tape.

SARAH   You've got it?

CHRIS   He sent it this morning. (SARAH RAISES AN EYEBROW) It's good.

CHAD   And it doesn't say where he's buried? (SARAH GLARES AT HIM) What? I'm just asking!

SARAH   I need you to send me your copy. I'll get it to Al. Al, how long's the New York piece again?

AL   Two forty.

SARAH   And I need you to get down to the Vatican. If we run this, and I'm saying it's an 'if', we're gonna do two on the piece and forty live from the Vatican. Alright?

GARETH   (OFF) Alright.

SARAH   Alright. And I don't have to tell you not to talk to absolutely anyone on this, do I?

GARETH   (OFF) Don't worry.

SARAH   It's my job to worry.

GARETH   (OFF) Yeah.

SARAH STABS THE PHONE OFF.

JOSIE   What just happened?

AL   We killed Jesus.

SARAH   Alright…

BRUCE   You're not seriously thinking about running this?

SARAH   I need…

BRUCE   I'm talking to you Sarah!

SARAH   And I heard you Bruce but it's a little under an hour to air and I don't have a ten written yet. I need to let…

BRUCE   There's no way corporate will…

SARAH   Bruce! Focus! I need you and David in hair. I need Chris to pull the footage, I need Josie to tell us the sky's not falling and I need Al to write me at least two versions of the ten! Got it? I'll listen to argument but there's no point talking this over 'til we know if it's airable! I'll look at it and we'll discuss it, but right now I've got a news show to make. Alright? (TO CHRIS) Chris, put the footage to my desktop. I'll look at it there and I'll need you to man this one yourself, I don't want this getting out til we know what it is. David, get down to hair and makeup then get back here as quick as you can. Al. I need every story and this one.

AL   You'd run it second?

SARAH   I don't know where I'd run it yet. But if I have to do the death of Christmas I'm not doing Bethlehem at the same time.

PEOPLE START PACKING UP, GETTING READY TO MOVE.

AL   Got it.

SARAH   Bruce. Hang back, would you?

EXIT DAVID, JOSIE, AND AL.

CHAD   You want me to work with Chris?

SARAH   I want you… I want you to go wait in the corridor, alright? I've got to talk to Bruce then I've got something important I need you to do, alright?

CHAD   Important?

SARAH   Double oh, important.

CHAD   (PUT OUT) Alright.

EXIT CHAD.

SARAH   Chris. Who's on camera?

CHRIS   Brown and Murphy.

SARAH   Alright. Put Brown on one. If we do this…

CHRIS   Yeah.

SARAH   And you're gonna have to write the cue…

CHRIS   Look at what we've got.

SARAH   Yeah.

CHRIS   I'll send it to your desktop.

SARAH   Yeah. Thanks. What do you think?

CHRIS   I think I'm glad it's not my call.

SARAH   Yeah. Get to work.

EXIT CHRIS.

BRUCE   You can't run this.

SARAH   Bruce…

BRUCE   There's no way Alan's gonna let you run this and you know it.

SARAH   Bruce, I swear to God, the best way to convince me of something is not by threatening me. I don't know if we're running it.

BRUCE   You can't.

SARAH   I don't know. But, and I need you to listen… Okay. Look. I know we're not on the same page here, and I know that you need, or you feel you need, to place distance between us at the moment and I can understand that, I can. But this is my room. Mine. When they kick me out they kick me out but until then there's just one voice here and that's mine.

BRUCE   You can't run this.

SARAH   And I'm saying I don't know, but I'm saying it's my decision to make. Don't ever try to walk out on me again and don't ever tell me what I can or can't do, alright?

BRUCE   That it?

SARAH   That's it.

BRUCE   I'm not kidding about the story.

SARAH   I know. Just… get down to wardrobe, give me time to look at it and we'll take it from there. Alright?

BRUCE   Yeah.

EXIT BRUCE.

SARAH STANDS OVER THE DESK, BREATHS DEEPLY, AND SLAMS THE TABLE WITH HER FIST, SENDING PAPERS FLYING.

SARAH   Damn it!

END OF ACT 1.

The Last Christmas

ACT 2

ACT II

SCENE 1

LIGHTS UP ON SARAH, STANDING EXACTLY AS BEFORE, MERE SECONDS LATER, ALONE IN THE ROOM.

ENTER CHAD.

CHAD	You fire him?
SARAH	(STRAIGHTENING) What?
CHAD	Did you fire him?
SARAH	What do you want, Chad?
CHAD	You asked me to wait in the hall.
SARAH	Yeah?
CHAD	Double oh, secret stuff.

HE HANDS HER A BRANDED COFFEE.

SARAH	What's this.
CHAD	Soy decaf.

SARAH LOOKS AT HIM AND DRINKS.

SARAH	(SURPRISED, SMILING) So it is.
CHAD	What you asked for.
SARAH	(PAUSE) You know your uncle well?
CHAD	You could say that.
SARAH	Yeah? What kind of man's he strike you as?
CHAD	I guess that depends upon who you ask. But if you want to know who he's going to side with, you or the poster boy for right-wing politics, I'd tell you to start updating your resume.
SARAH	Yeah, that's what I thought.
CHAD	You gonna run it?
SARAH	I don't know.
CHAD	I think you do.

SARAH   Don't push it.

CHAD   How does it work?

SARAH   Sorry.

CHAD   How does it work, what goes on the air?

SARAH   Jesus, I don't know. A number of things.

CHAD   What CNN runs with?

SARAH   Sometimes. Sometimes it's what CNN's not.

CHAD   On the nine.

SARAH   Yes, on the nine.

CHAD   Bet you, most mornings, you listen to the radio on the way in and run with it from there. Bet you most of the time they're getting it from one of the twenty-four hour broadcasts, who, no doubt, are just getting it from the internet.

SARAH   That what you think?

CHAD   That's why it's so, I don't know, uniform? I mean, what? We've got something like four hundred national reporters, another two overseas and what do we run with? Paris Hilton's sex tape… which we got off a blog.

SARAH   If you think that's how it works, why are you here?

CHAD   Istanbul. Pfizer. Nigeria.

SARAH   No one likes a kiss ass, Chad.

CHAD   Three stories no one was running before you picked up on them.

SARAH   Tell your uncle that.

CHAD   I have.

SARAH   (REALLY LOOKING AT HIM) Alright. Tell me. Would you run it?

CHAD   If it's there?

SARAH   Yes.

CHAD   No.

SARAH   Champion of the underdog!

CHAD   I'm rich, Sarah. I like it!

SARAH   Yeah.

CHAD   It's…

SARAH   No, seriously. I don't get that. I don't. Look, you say we run what everyone else runs?

CHAD   Don't want to lose the share.

SARAH   Don't want to lose the share. So, whatever gets the most hits runs.

CHAD   We'll always have Paris.

SARAH   How is that any different from what you're saying?

CHAD   I don't follow.

SARAH   You're rich. Don't lose it. Don't piss off daddy…

CHAD   Uncle.

SARAH   Don't piss off Uncle Alan. Keep your head in the trough, nose to the food,

CHAD   Where as you?

SARAH   Keep the market share. Don't rock the boat. Maintain audience. Build revenue.

CHAD   People want what they want.

SARAH   People want what I tell them.

CHAD   True.

SARAH   You know, Japan. Three agricultural ministers last year. Three. You know why? Each one was siphoning off tax funds for their own private purposes. One even managed to commit suicide. You know what happened to the other two?

CHAD   Nothing?

SARAH   Nothing. They just quit. No jail. No returned funds.

CHAD   You think that's all this is?

SARAH   It's fraud!

CHAD   You think this is just going to get brushed under the carpet?

SARAH   Why not?

CHAD   Then why run it?

SARAH   Because it's news! We're not the police. We're a news station.

CHAD   It might even help the market share!

SARAH   But you wouldn't run it.

CHAD   Not in a million years.

SARAH   Because you think I'll lose my job. My nose in the thing.

CHAD   You've got to be in it, to win it.

SARAH   Yeah.

THE PHONE RINGS. SARAH PICKS IT UP, LISTENS, THEN PUTS IT DOWN BEFORE GOING TO HER COMPUTER.

CHAD   That Chris?

SARAH   So… I've got to watch this.

CHAD   I'll watch it with you.

SARAH   No, Valerie. Rich boys don't get to play in the mud. They might get their hands dirty and tarnish the silver.

CHAD   It must suck being you.

SARAH   I'm good at it.

CHAD   And the double oh, stuff.

SARAH   Hmm?

CHAD   Before, the whole, important stuff thing. In the corridor?

SARAH   (REMEMBERING) Right. Yes. Listen. And this is important, alright.

CHAD   Okay.

SARAH   What do men want?

CHAD   Seriously? A longer hockey season.

SARAH   For Christmas.

CHAD   Good will and peace to all men. No, wait, that might just be women.

SARAH   If it was for a story.

CHAD   I don't know. Something personal.

SARAH   Excellent. Here's what I want you to do. (SHE THROWS HIM HER PURSE) Scour the land for something. A Christmas present. Something a husband might want from his wife.

CHAD   You're kidding me.

SARAH   Something that might be considered personal.

CHAD   This… You're kidding me. You didn't get David anything.

SARAH   How'd you know we were married?

CHAD   Seriously?

SARAH   I did but…

CHAD   It wasn't personal?

SARAH   Just, get something, alright? I'm hopeless at this kind of thing.

CHAD   For your husband?

SARAH   If it's not too much trouble.

CHAD   On Christmas Day?

SARAH   You were so good with the coffee.

CHAD THINKS ABOUT IT FOR A WHILE THEN TAKES THE PURSE OFF HER.

CHAD   Goddamn it.

SARAH   Thank you, C. I'll make sure your uncle knows how well you're doing.

CHAD   Coming from you, that might not help.

SARAH   Thank you!

EXIT CHAD.

SARAH SITS AT THE DESK, STARING AT HER COMPUTER SCREEN. UNSEEN, SHE WATCHES THE FOOTAGE FROM

ROME. WE CAN HEAR THE SOUND OF AN AUDIO FILE BUT NOT CLEARLY ENOUGH TO MAKE IT OUT.

WHEN THE FILE ENDS SHE RETURNS IT TO THE BEGINNING.

JOSIE ENTERS STAGE RIGHT, MOVING AROUND THE CONFERENCE TABLE AND ENTERING SARAH'S OFFICE. SEEING HER COMING SARAH CLOSES THE FILE AND LOWERS THE LAPTOP SCREEN.

JOSIE KNOCKS AND ENTERS.

JOSIE   You got that minute now?

SARAH   (UNSURE) Sure. What's up?

JOSIE   It's about Al. The party last night…

SARAH   Yeah. I noticed there was something.

JOSIE   I think I need to make a claim.

SARAH   A claim?

JOSIE   You know. Sexual harassment?

THE TWO WOMEN LOOK AT EACH OTHER.

SARAH   Are you sure?

JOSIE   Pretty sure, yeah.

SARAH   I mean, you're sure it was harassment. Not just sexual.

JOSIE   Of course!

SARAH   I mean, honest-to-god sexual harassment, not, you know, "god you look hot!" Because you do. Look hot. You do. And if it was just that and not something else then do you think it's something we can, you know, get back to.

JOSIE   It was.

SARAH   Cos, I mean. There isn't a worse time.

JOSIE   He put his thing in my hand.

SARAH   Where was your hand at the time?

JOSIE   On my leg.

THE TWO WOMEN LOOK AT EACH OTHER AGAIN. THIS TIME IT'S SARAH WHO BREAKS, COMING AROUND THE DESK.

SARAH   I'm sorry. Really. It's… well. Are you alright?

JOSIE   I'm fine.

SARAH   Yeah?

JOSIE   Well…

SARAH   Okay.

JOSIE   It's just that I think, you know, he shouldn't be allowed to do that, you know?

SARAH   He's not. Of course he's not. He won't be. I mean… (SHE LOOKS AT THE CLOCK) He isn't. I promise. You were right to come to me with this. He was wrong, really, really wrong to do that. That kind of thing has no place… What I'm saying is. There's, you know. Protocol about these things. Corporate has to get involved and it's Christmas and we're up against it.

JOSIE   I understand.

SARAH   We'll do something about it. I promise. He was wrong and I'm sorry. But I just need to get through the next ninety minutes, you know?

JOSIE   I understand.

SARAH   Good. I hope so. You okay?

JOSIE   (MOTIONING TO THE COMPUTER) Is it real?

SARAH   Yeah. Yeah, I think it is. Well, real enough to run anyway.

JOSIE   Can we do that?

SARAH   Sure. We're a news division and this is news.

JOSIE   Think we should?

SARAH   That… That I'm not sure of.

JOSIE   Bruce won't go for it.

SARAH   Tell me something I don't know.

JOSIE   And corporate?

SARAH   Aren't you supposed to be in hair?

JOSIE   They've got two girls down there and I go on last so…

SARAH   Right. I'd better get back to…

JOSIE   Yeah.

SARAH   We'll do something about it. I promise.

JOSIE   Just not today.

SARAH   I need him for the next ninety.

JOSIE   You know. There's this thing. Personally and professionally. I mean. I'm pretty, I dress well. I must want it, you know what I mean?

SARAH   It doesn't work like that, I promise.

JOSIE   And then there's the 'weather girl' thing. I'm a weather girl so I must a) be dumb and b) want it.

SARAH   It doesn't work like that.

JOSIE   I have a degree in meteorology!

SARAH   And I can't even pronounce it.

JOSIE   I'm not stupid.

SARAH   And you're not an object. I promise. We'll get to this. Really.

JOSIE   You need him.

SARAH   For the next ninety? Yes. Yes, I do, God, help me.

ENTER DAVID.

JOSIE   Yeah.

DAVID COMES IN, FRESH FROM MAKEUP. A NEW SHIRT AND TIE WITH HIS COLLAR PROTECTED BY TISSUE PAPER.

HE DOESN'T BOTHER TO KNOCK.

SARAH   (TO JOSIE) We'll get to it. I promise.

EXIT JOSIE.

DAVID   (TO JOSIE) Hey. (TO SARAH) Get to what?

SARAH   Close the door.

DAVID   You've looked at it?

SARAH RAISES THE LID OF THE LAPTOP AGAIN.

SARAH   He's good. I mean. He's covered just about everything you possibly can. He's gonna either get a Nobel or burnt at the stake.

DAVID   It's real?

SARAH   Real enough to run. Yes. I mean, shit, the papers could be fakes. The priest could be, well...

DAVID   We're sure he's a real priest?

SARAH   He's listed on the Vatican website. Photo and everything.

DAVID   The Vatican have a website?

SARAH   Vatican dot 'va'.

DAVID   Wow!

SARAH   That's one word for it. He's got it. It's a story. I don't see how we can't.

DAVID   And you think they'll let you?

SUDDENLY SARAH IS ALL BUSINESS. SHE SNAPS SHUT THE LAPTOP AGAIN AND GLARES AT DAVID, THINKING.

SARAH   So... Listen. What you were saying before? I need it.

DAVID   What?

SARAH   Whatever it is you have on Bruce.

DAVID   Now?

SARAH   I need to have it in my ammo.

DAVID   You said you didn't want it?

SARAH   (ANGER GROWING) And now I'm saying I do. If I've got to go toe-to-toe with that bastard over th...

42

DAVID   Hang on. You'd use it?

SARAH   I don't know.

DAVID   Honey, look. I know you're in a tight spot. I mean, shit, an hour ago I was ready to use it myself, but for this..?

SARAH   I said I don't know!

DAVID   And I'm saying there are battles and there are battles, but this? You get him, what about corporate?

SARAH   Screw corporate!

DAVID   And you think he's just not going to call them.

SARAH   I just need to know. For now. Alright?

DAVID   (PONDERING) I don't know.

SARAH   David. (SHE FIDDLES WITH HER WEDDING RING) I wouldn't ask…

DAVID   He's married.

SARAH   Married?

DAVID   England. Five years ago.

ENTER AL.

ACROSS THE CONFERENCE ROOM, AL ENTERS, PAPERS IN HAND.

SARAH   Really?

DAVID   Yeah.

SARAH   Really?

DAVID   Sarah. You can't run it. You know that?

SARAH   (TO AL AS HE ENTERS) What you got there, Al?

AL   (HANDING THE PAPERS TO SARAH) Copy.

SARAH   (LOOKING AT THE PAPERS) Already?

AL   Thing writes itself.

SARAH   And the other thing?

AL   Next page.

DAVID   How's the head?

AL   (SITTING) Feels like a bear shat in my throat.

DAVID   Yeah?

SARAH   You watched it?

AL   I skimmed. You know the thing I can't get is how stupid they were. I mean, here we are, two thousand years of secrets blotted out because someone doesn't know what CC means.

DAVID   Carbon copy.

AL   Really?

DAVID   Think so. What it used to mean before everything went electronic.

AL   Sarah? Your husband's old.

SARAH   This is good. I want to change the pejorative in the second paragraph. Move it to passive and we shouldn't have a problem.

AL   (QUOTING) "The discovery has been made despite attempts to keep it from the general public and ecclesiastic scholars alike." 'Pejoratively'. Yeah, that'll work.

SARAH   David doesn't think we should run the thing.

AL   Really?

DAVID   I'm not saying we shouldn't run it, I'm saying that we're not.

AL   Come on!

DAVID   Look… I think there's a lot that's gone on here over the last six months that's unfair. Hypocritical even. And I don't think there's anyone in this room right now that thinks otherwise. And we are where we are. But to run this to get back at corporate? Come on! And Bruce is right. It's Christmas.

AL   (SHOUTING) Come on! Ow. (HE WINCES AT THE NOISE IN HIS HEAD AND DROPS HIS VOICE) Come on. It's got nothing to do with this! We ran what we ran and that's it. We're a goddamned news show!

DAVID   Don't give… Listen. You write the news. Get it? You write the goddamned news! Not the reporters. You, most of the time.

AL   So?

DAVID   It's scripted. That the way it's supposed to be? Cute little asides on cue cards? "That's right Bruce, I've met your mother and I think she'd be the first to join us in saying Merry Christmas to all our troops. Keep that eggnog coming Mrs. B."

AL   What's your point, David?

DAVID   I'm saying I'm old. And I'm done. When Sarah goes, I go. (SARAH IS TAKEN ABACK BY THIS NEWS) I've been doing this a long time, but let's be honest with ourselves. We're not a news show, we're show news. There's three major wars out there at the moment and only one of them's gonna get any kind of cover. We've got twenty minutes and they've got ten covering pageants so, let's not pretend this is anything other than what it is. An attempt to go out in a blaze of glory. All guns firing! And this?

AL   You don't believe it?

DAVID   What's to believe? No. It's all there alright. It is what it is. But to run a story like this without at least checking more thoroughly? One hour after you get it? One hour before air? Let's not pretend it's anything other than what it is.

SARAH   And what is it?

DAVID   A chance to get back at the right. A chance to show the Christian right that they can force you off the network but they can't keep you quiet. A blaze of glory!

SARAH   Gee honey. What is it you're accusing me of? A lack of professionalism or religious bigotry.

DAVID   Say what you like…

SARAH   I will! That's twice in the last hour someone's accused me of being a Jew!

DAVID   Say what you like…

AL   It's not really an accusation though, is it?

DAVID   Say what you like! But this story. It's not gonna run. Two minutes from now Bruce is gonna walk in here and five minutes after that, if he hasn't already, he's gonna call Tom over at corporate or Alan even and there'll be no story. Not then. So you guys keep talking about it, saying what you want about it, but that second page better be complete because that's what we're going to go with.

THE ROOM IS SILENT FOR A SECOND.

SARAH   I married you, didn't I.

DAVID   So?

SARAH   You're a goyim.

AL   You know what I've never understood about Jews?

SARAH   What?

AL   Why is it the only race with a religion named after it. I mean, you can convert to it, can't you? So what do you say? I'm Jewish but I'm not Jewish if you catch my drift.

SARAH   I think it's called Judaism.

AL   Yeah, but you never hear a Rabbi saying, you know. "Vengeance is not Judaish?" Do you?

DAVID   Shut up, Al.

AL   Shutting up.

SARAH   You never said that before.

DAVID   What?

SARAH   The leaving thing.

DAVID   Well.

SARAH   Yeah.

ENTER BRUCE.

BRUCE ENTERS FROM ACROSS THE CONFERENCE ROOM. SARAH PICKS UP THE PHONE AND STABS NUMBERS.

BRUCE   Have we dropped it yet?

SARAH   Hang on. (INTO THE PHONE) Chris? Yeah, how you coming with the video? Yeah. Okay. Mind coming down here for five minutes. No. Now, if that's okay. I'd like a senior staff.

SHE HANGS UP.

BRUCE   We're not still on it, are we?

SARAH   Hang on, Bruce. I'd like to get everyone down here before we get into something.

BRUCE   (SITTING) Fine.

AL   And another thing. Hanukkah! I mean what is that?
It's not even the most important day on the Jewish calendar!

DAVID   Neither's Christmas.

AL   Really?

SARAH   Easter.

AL   Let's run it at Easter then!

BRUCE   What's he talking about?

DAVID   Al's becoming anti-Semitic.

AL   Well, you did kill Christ.

DAVID   Apparently not.

AL   Point.

SARAH   Jesus!

BRUCE   You know. If you wouldn't mind not taking the
Lord's name in vain during this conversation.

SARAH   You're kidding me?

AL   You do do it a lot.

BRUCE   It's offensive.

SARAH   (PAUSE) Fine. Whatever. (PAUSE) You know…
never mind.

DAVID   Say it.

AL   What?

SARAH   Don't worry about it.

DAVID   Say it.

SARAH   I'd rather not. Okay?

DAVID   She's an atheist.

SARAH   David…

AL   I thought you were Jewish?!

SARAH   I am Jewish!

DAVID   She just doesn't believe in it.

SARAH   I believe in some of it.

BRUCE   You're not practicing?

AL   You wear white after Labour Day!

SARAH   (TO BRUCE) How long… (TO AL) What? (TO BRUCE) How long have we known each other?

BRUCE   Somethings you don't ask.

DAVID   You got that right!

AL   You're not Judaish, then.

SARAH   You see a mezuzah on the doorposts? You see me wandering around laying tefillin? You hear me muttering the Shema between segments?

AL   Gesundheit.

SARAH   I believe what I believe, okay? And while we're at it, I don't see any of you kneeling in prayer before the show, or whatever it is you're supposed to do. So, can we please keep this on a professional level, okay, and not keep running off on little crusades?

BRUCE   Fine by me.

ENTER CHRIS.

CHRIS ENTERS ACROSS THE CONFERENCE ROOM. SARAH WAVES AT HER TO ENTER.

SARAH   Alright. We all know what we're here for. I'd like to go round the room. I've looked at it and what we've got; it's there. I mean. We've run with a lot less for a lot more.

AL   Yeah, but Bush could only kill us. God can send us to hell.

SARAH   I want to know why we shouldn't run the piece and I want to know now. And, I swear to God, one of you makes one comment (SHE POINTS AT AL) joking or otherwise about my race having anything to do with this at all and I'll fire you, here and now. Got it?

BRUCE   Alright, I'll make this simple. You can't run it.

SARAH   Why not?

BRUCE   Because it's wrong!

SARAH   It's not! We've got hard copy evidence. We've got interviews… Is this the body of Christ or is this not the body of Christ? I don't know! But I do know that that's what the Church believes and that's what they've been covering up for the last two thousand years.

BRUCE   I don't mean it's wrong. I mean it's wrong. Morally! And for the sake of this conversation I think we'd better call it the Catholic Church or Rome, because I know a lot of evangelicals who are going to deny this.

CHRIS   How?

BRUCE   By faith! The power of believing in something unseen? I don't care if we run DNA tests on the Turin shroud and find it an exact match. Mostly everyone in the Christian community is going to say it's not true!

SARAH   So? Last year they ran a conference in Iran claiming that the Holocaust didn't happen and over five thousand people turned up. Doesn't change history. People can choose to believe what they want to believe. We're not saying they can't. But this is news!

BRUCE   So was the actress.

SARAH   Oh, come on!

AL   What?

CHRIS   He's saying that what's-her-name panties…

BRUCE   I know what I'm saying. The actress was news, it was, and you choose not to run with that. How is this any different?

DAVID   It is though.

BRUCE   People who believe are better than people who don't.

PAUSE.

SARAH   I don't even know what that means.

BRUCE   People who believe are better than people who don't! You want me to line up the long list of humanitarian atheists for you?

SARAH   What did I just say about…

AL   And this has something to do with it, how?

SARAH   People are people, Bruce. They don't need to believe
in a deity to do something good.

CHRIS   Game theory.

BRUCE   Tell that to the… Tell that to people working with
AIDS victims. Tell that to the priests who work in some of the poorest
areas…

SARAH   And you think they're gonna stop because we run
this?

AL   Exactly when did we start getting syndicated in
Calcutta?

DAVID   I think this is getting off the point.

BRUCE   Which is?

SARAH   It's fraud!

AL   She's right.

SARAH   It's fraud!

BRUCE   I'm sorry. I don't see it.

SARAH   How? What are you… How can you not see this!

BRUCE   Faith supersedes fact. Simple. The entirety of any
religion is not based on facts surrounding its advent. It's about what
happened afterwards.

SARAH   Well, woopty-do for Mr. Zen.

DAVID   Sarah..!

SARAH   The Catholic Church is worth, what? Several billion
dollars worldwide? And a good amount of that was collected from
people because they didn't know that the people they were giving the
money to had a good faith basis to believe that the whole thing wasn't
a crock of shit!

BRUCE   And again! The foundation of belief is not fact!

SARAH   We sued tobacco. We're doing it now! Not because cigarettes kill but because the heads of the companies knew they did and lied about it.

BRUCE   Oh, come on!

SARAH   These are facts, they're reported and we've backed them up. That's news. End of story.

BRUCE   Since when did that matter?

AL   Come on!

BRUCE   No. Seriously. Since when did that matter?

SARAH   Since I took over the show, that's when.

BRUCE   Really? Whatever happened to it bleeds, it leads?

DAVID   9/11 happened to it.

BRUCE   Exactly! Now it's whatever frightens or makes you forget that runs!

DAVID   I'm with Bruce on this.

BRUCE   Yes, they brought you in to sharpen up the news. Yes, you did a good job for a while. But let's not pretend that we don't have an agenda. That you don't have an agenda!

SARAH   And you don't?

BRUCE   To what's right? Yes. You run this story and what's it going to prove? What? It's going to divide the Church. It's going to divide the country. It's already dividing this show!

AL   Not exactly hard to do.

BRUCE   It's going to pluralize everyone. The right, the left. Everyone! You run this story and you're enticing a riot. At Christmas! I mean, like people were going to take it well at any other time of the year, but at Christmas!

CHRIS   If we don't run it, someone else will!

BRUCE   Then let them! Let this fall at their door! Let The New Yorker or someone do a piece on it. We're a major network with principles, family principles, to uphold!

AL   Oh, bullshit!

51

BRUCE   You want to be the one who wrote the 'killed Christ' article, go ahead, but not on my news show!

SARAH   It's not your news!

AL   And there it is, isn't it! You just don't want to be the one who comes out and says it, do you? It's not that you think this is morally wrong, it's that you think it's a bad career move. Right? This thing has Pulitzer all over it!

BRUCE   So what? Yes. Yes, I'm worried about my career and you should be too, but I'm more worried about the effect this will have on our society!

AL   Bullshit! It's all self, self, self.

BRUCE   (TO SARAH) And no. I don't give a damn about the Pulitzer. This is wrong, and I'm having nothing to do with it.

AL   And you call yourself a journalist!

BRUCE   I don't. Actually. I'm not! I'm not a journalist. I've never pretended to be. I'm a presenter! I present the news! You think I don't know the difference? But this is me telling you I'm not presenting this.

SARAH   Chris?

CHRIS   I don't know. I mean. This is the biggest story since... what?

SARAH   9/11.

BRUCE   And we did such a bang up job reporting that!

CHRIS   Which is the point, isn't it? I mean, why didn't we report everything. The bin Ladins leaving the country... everything? We knew it was happening? Right? We just didn't want to get involved. We didn't want to go against the grain, so we kept our mouths shut.

BRUCE   This isn't the same.

CHRIS   We didn't report it because we didn't want trouble. How's that any different from this? I'm sorry, but I say we don't run this, with what we have, then we're cowards. All of us. And we deserve every bad rating we've ever got.

SARAH   Alright. Let's take a vote on it.

BRUCE   Can I just ask why Josie isn't involved here.

AL   The weather girl?

BRUCE   And why he's even still employed at this office?

SARAH   Josie's not here because she's in hair. And I haven't got time. We're voting now. Al?

AL   Run it.

SARAH   Chris?

CHRIS   Yeah.

BRUCE   This is ridiculous.

SARAH   Bruce?

BRUCE   No. Of course no. No.

SARAH   David?

DAVID   (SOTTO) No.

SARAH   Sorry?

DAVID   Sorry. No.

SARAH   Alright. And I say yes. We run it.

BRUCE   I think you kept Josie out of this room so that the vote would go your way. And I think you kept him (HE POINTS TO AL) in a job for the very same reason.

SARAH   Josie's in hair and even if she weren't, I'm producer of this show and therefore get the majority ruling. Now, I've listened to argument. We're running the piece. Chris, I want you to make sure we're set in the control room. Work with Al on any time constraints. Al, (SHE HOLDS UP THE PAGES) get this on the prompter. Bruce...

BRUCE   (STANDING) I'm sorry, Sarah. I think I have to go over you to corporate on this one.

SARAH   There's a surprise. The rest of you, we're live in (SHE LOOKS AT THE CLOCK; DEPENDING ON THE TIME HER ANSWER WILL BE DIFFERENT) thirty-four minutes. Do what you do.

CHRIS   Want me to run tape on the other one.

SARAH   (PAUSE) Do what you think you have to.

EXIT CHRIS, AL, AND DAVID.

BRUCE   (INTO THE PHONE) I'm gonna need the home numbers for either Tom Philander or Alan Smith. (PAUSE) Yes, I realise the time. This is Bruce Baxter with the nine a.m. news and I'm going to need either phone number or both if that's possible. (HE TAKES A PEN FROM A POCKET AND JOTS DOWN THE NUMBERS) No. That's fine. I'll get them on my mobile.

SARAH CLOSES THE DOOR TO HER OFFICE.

BLACKOUT FOR TEN SECONDS.

END OF SCENE.

SCENE 2

LIGHTS UP ON SARAH, ALONE IN HER OFFICE. SHE
STANDS AT THE DOOR, LOOKING OUT INTO THE
CONFERENCE ROOM, WEIGHING HER OPTIONS.

CLOCK READS 08:32.

DAVID ENTERS FROM THE ROOM, DRESSED AS BEFORE.
SEEING HIM SARAH TURNS HER BACK TOWARDS HIM
BUT DOESN'T ENTER THE OFFICE AGAIN, STAYING IN
THE DOORWAY, HER ANGER GROWING.

DAVID   Alan's down in the studio. Talking to Chris.

SARAH   Yeah.

DAVID   What did you think he was gonna do?

SARAH   You could have backed me up a bit in there!

DAVID   Is that what this is?

SARAH   I don't know how you can side with him on this.

DAVID   I'm not siding with anyone! Least of all Bruce.

SARAH   He's the one who took your spot.

DAVID   He didn't... Sarah, look...

SARAH   You can say it.

DAVID   Years ago. Back when I was at ABC the first time.
Before the BBC. I was... well, I was this huge pain in the ass back then.
I mean it was me, Ted Koppel, Eric Sevareid and Chet. I was a reporter.
Me and Ted. But you know, I'd got a few good stories and was making
my way through the fast track.

SARAH   I know all this.

DAVID   (IGNORING HER) But I made a mistake. See, I
had a choice. A piece of mine was being pulled. It was a piece about a
coal mine. Black lung. And I thought, no, I knew it was good story.

SARAH   I've heard you tell this before.

DAVID   Then you'll hear it one more time. They pulled the
story. I swear, I can't even remember the reason any more, but they
pulled the story. And I was, you know, I was livid. Who were they to

55

tell me what was a good story or not? Who were they to say whether it was relevant?

SARAH   You blew up at them and Huntley fired you.

DAVID   I blew up at them and they fired me. But what I didn't tell you before, is that I knew it. I knew it. I knew when I went into that office that it would cost me my job. My career. I knew but I did it anyway. I pushed the button. I knew it. And I didn't care.

SARAH   And that's what you think I'm doing now?

DAVID   I think there's something of that in each of us. We want to destroy ourselves so that people can save us and we can feel, what? Loved? Valued?

SARAH   It's an important story!

DAVID   Yes. Yes it is. But I don't think you care about any of that. I don't. I think you want to explode your career so that you can prove to yourself that you're worth it!

SARAH   Jesus, you talk shit.

DAVID   Do I?

SARAH   You were there. Three months ago! You were with me on that! When that thing went live…

DAVID   I went to the mat for you on that! We all did.

SARAH   It was the right thing to do!

DAVID   It was. It was. But we lost. We lost and they're gonna let you go. Maybe not 'til April but we all know they're not going to renew. It was the right fight, we fought it, we lost and no one is more angry about that than me.

SARAH   You know what it was about!

DAVID   I do. Yes. A left-wing liberal looks good on paper but marrying the chair? It was never going to happen and we should have seen it coming. I was with you on that.

SARAH   But not on this.

DAVID   Not any more, no.

SARAH   It's an important story.

DAVID   So let someone tell it. Let corporate cut it, get on the phone and leak the damn story to the New York Times. But that's not what you're going to do, is it?

SARAH   Why am I the only one who seems to get this? We're a news program, we…

DAVID   Stop it. Just… Just, stop it. You married a man twenty years your senior and, trust me, I'm as happy about that as I can be, but I'm not going to watch you end your career just as it was getting started. Ten years from now you're going to be running a news division for CNN, NBC, the top three.

SARAH   Al Jazeera?

DAVID   But you do this, it's over. Really. And I'm not going to just sit around and watch that happen.

SARAH   You think getting fired from here is going to hurt my chances?

DAVID   For this, yes! This! You joke but…

SARAH   It's an important story.

DAVID   And you're an important person. To me. Let corporate cut it. Give them a couple of rounds for show then take a dive.

SARAH   You think I'm going to use it.

DAVID   I think you're looking to be saved and there's no one here can do it.

SARAH   Even you.

DAVID   Especially me. Throw a couple of punches then take a dive.

SARAH   You know I didn't give you your Christmas present.

DAVID   The coffee machine?

SARAH   You know it?

DAVID   I signed for the damn thing. Very practical.

SARAH   I'm a practical person.

DAVID   Yes. Yes, you are.

SARAH	No. The other thing.
DAVID	What is it?
SARAH	It's a secret.
DAVID	Okay.
SARAH	Really. It's a secret. I have got one.

THE PHONE IN HER OFFICE RINGS. SARAH MOVES ACROSS TO THE DESK AND PICKS IT UP.

SARAH   (INTO THE PHONE) Yes. (PAUSE) I'll be right down. (SHE HANGS UP. TO DAVID) Alan wants me in the studio.

DAVID	Man loves that studio.
SARAH	Better not keep him waiting.
DAVID	Sarah?
SARAH	We've on air in thirty. This isn't covered by then…
DAVID	Sarah!
SARAH	I won't.
DAVID	Really?

SARAH   Look. I… I hate Bruce. I want to beat him. But… not like this.

DAVID	Alright.
SARAH	You'll be here?
DAVID	I'll be here.

SARAH KISSES HIM ON THE CHEEK.

SARAH	It makes the froth and everything.
DAVID	What does?
SARAH	The coffee maker.
DAVID	But you've got me something else.
SARAH	And the coffee maker!
DAVID	Espresso?
SARAH	The works.

DAVID   I got you underwear.

SARAH   I'll see you in a few.

DAVID   I'll be here.

EXIT SARAH.

DAVID SLUMPS INTO A CHAIR AND LOOKS WORRIEDLY AFTER HER.

END OF ACT II.

ACT 3

ACT III

SCENE 1

THE NEWS DESK.

LIGHTS UP ON A NEWS DESK IN A STUDIO. THE NEWS DESK, FAMILIAR TO ALL NEWS STUDIOS, IS BIG ENOUGH TO SIT TWO PEOPLE COMFORTABLY BEHIND IT AND HAS A LEDGE FOR PAPERS. A CORPORATE LOGO - CNB - IS ATTACHED TO THE FRONT OF THE DESK. BEHIND IT, A LARGE GREEN SCREEN TOWERS OVER THE SEATS.

ALAN STANDS AT THE FRONT OF THE DESK, PAPERS IN HAND, WAITING FOR SARAH.

A SIGN SAYS NO SMOKING. HE IS SMOKING A CIGARETTE.

ENTER CHAD.

CHAD ENTERS CARRYING A STORE BAG.

CHAD	Uncle Alan.
ALAN	Chad. What you got there?
CHAD	Honestly? Women's underwear.
ALAN	Well, don't let me stop you.
CHAD	You here about the Jesus thing?
ALAN	Let's not call it that, shall we?
CHAD	Okay.
ALAN	What are you doing here Chad?
CHAD	I'm interning, Uncle Alan. Remember?
ALAN	Is my house that bad?
CHAD	I'm sorry?
ALAN	Is my house that bad?
CHAD	Of course not.

ALAN   Yet I'm told by your mother that you've decided to start your internship one week early rather than sit down to dinner with me.

CHAD   It seemed the right thing to do, Uncle Alan.

ALAN   Did it?

CHAD   I just thought with everyone not here...

ALAN   I think you misunderstood me before so I'm going to ask again, Chad. What are you doing here?

CHAD   How exactly do you mean, Uncle Alan?

ALAN   Since when did you take an interest in the news business?

CHAD   I majored...

ALAN   You majored in art history, son. What? You think I don't check those little resumes that come across my desk? You think your mother doesn't talk to me? When I bought CNBC, you know what I bought if for?

CHAD   The sport.

ALAN   I bought it for the sport. This was before pay-per-view. This was before...

CHAD   Radio?

ALAN   (STEPPING FORWARD) I didn't catch that?

CHAD   (SHOCKED) Nothing.

ALAN   (PAUSE) I bought it for the sport. Now, we're the number three news division on the east coast. Number two in the heartland. And you know why?

CHAD   No, sir.

ALAN   Because I'm very, very careful about who I hire.

CHAD   Yes, Uncle Alan.

ALAN   This... what did you call it?

CHAD   Jesus thing?

ALAN   This yours?

CHAD   No, sir.

ALAN   Something to get back at me?

CHAD   No.

ALAN   Something to bite the hand that feeds you?

CHAD   No, sir.

ALAN   (PAUSE) You're a bright boy, Chad.

CHAD   Thank you, Uncle Alan. I try.

ALAN   Ha. No. That's the one thing you never do. You're a bright boy Chad. Your mother was bright. But you know what bright gets you?

CHAD   A scholarship?

ALAN   A smart mouth, Chad. Nothing more. You're on a Damocles' sword, son.

CHAD   I'm sorry.

ALAN   It means…

CHAD   I know what it means.

ALAN   You rely on me. You rely on me and I don't like you.

CHAD   I'm sorry to hear that, Uncle Alan.

ALAN   You're a bright boy and you rely on me. You might even want me to like you. But, and here's the thing, the only way I'm ever going to like you is if you either stop being bright, or stop relying on me. Which of those do you think's more likely? (LONG PAUSE. THE TWO MEN STARE AT EACH OTHER) Your mother says you're not planning to make it for dinner?

CHAD   It's just with my first day…

ALAN   Make it.

CHAD   Yes, Uncle Alan.

ALAN   Now go give those panties to someone who can use them.

SARAH ENTERS FROM BEHIND THE AUDIENCE, CROSSING DOWN AS THOUGH CROSSING A STUDIO. WITH A NOD TO ALAN SHE STEPS ONTO THE STAGE. CHAD MOVES TOWARDS HER, HOLDS OUT THE BAG AND SHE TAKES IT.

CHAD   Here.

EXIT CHAD.

SARAH   Alan.

ALAN   Sarah. Hear you've got yourself in a little bit of
trouble.

SARAH   I wouldn't say that.

ALAN   Really. What would you say?

SARAH   It's news.

ALAN   Tell me about it. But the thing is, see. I don't pay you
to run a news studio so I can get dragged out of bed at eight a.m. on
Christmas Day. Shit, I haven't been out of bed on Christmas morning
since the kids were, well, kids.

SARAH   And I'm sorry about that. It wasn't my call.

ALAN   Of course it's your call. It's what I pay you for! If
you can't handle a disagreement within your own team then you don't
deserve to run a team. Follow? I pay you so I don't have to goddamned
do it myself, understand? My wife is in bed, waiting for me!

SARAH   Yes, sir.

ALAN   You've met my wife?

SARAH   I have indeed.

ALAN   Then you'll understand why I'm eager to get back
to her.

SARAH   These were exceptional circumstances.

ALAN   Yes, they were. Yes, they were. How long we got til
air?

SARAH   Fifteen minutes, give or take.

ALAN   (LOOKING AT THE PAPERS) You know, I've
been going to church since I was twelve.

SARAH   Yes, sir.

ALAN   And I can't make head nor tail of any of this. You?

SARAH   Umm, well. I mean. It's kind of all there.

ALAN   Explain it to me.

SARAH   You saw the tape?

ALAN   I want you to explain it to me.

SARAH   I'm… They found Jesus' body. (SHE LAUGHS) You know, when you say it like that it sounds ridiculous.

ALAN   You think millions of people's faith is something to laugh at?

SARAH   (STOPPING ABRUPTLY) No, sir.

ALAN   No, sir. So?

SARAH   So? They've… I don't know what they've got. I don't know what it means, but I know this. If that was the government. If the government had, I don't know, been covering up the fact that, say, cancer was caused by coffee or something, you think we'd be talking about sitting on it?

ALAN   Religion is cancer?

SARAH   I didn't say that.

ALAN   Just Christianity.

SARAH   No, sir.

ALAN   I love this studio.

SARAH   I know that you do.

ALAN   I started out in news. I tell you that?

SARAH   Yes, sir. You did.

ALAN   Print, but basically, it's the same thing. (PAUSE) You know what a smart man once told me? He told me news was like women. You might think this one's the one, but there's always another one that'll kill you, down the line. You barely get finished before another one's on the horizon.

SARAH   I wouldn't know.

ALAN   (PAUSE) You're Jewish, right?

SARAH   I don't see what that's got to do…

ALAN   Really?

SARAH   Really!

ALAN   You're a news director and you can't see how that may affect the story?

SARAH   No, sir!

ALAN   So, say they found proof. Just say. Say they found proof that Jesus was the messiah. That you guys had been getting it wrong for the last two thousand years. Would you run that?

SARAH   For a start, I find the term 'you guys' pretty offensive.

ALAN   Tough. Answer the question. Would you report it?

SARAH   You know, to everyone else, fine. I'm Jewish. I was born Jewish, but nobody's even stopped to ask what I believe!

ALAN   Lady, I couldn't give a rat's ass if you believe flying saucers are about to fly out of my butt and save the world. Answer the question!

SARAH   If they, if 'someone' had been covering it up. Yes. Yes I would. This is fraud.

ALAN   This isn't fraud.

SARAH   This is fraud! The Catholic Church...

ALAN   Sells a lot of shit. They all do! (BEAT) You know what always gets it for me, allegory-wise? The Tower of Babel.

SARAH   I'm sorry?

ALAN   The Tower of Babel. Genesis; I think. Group of people build a tower up into the sky and God smites them because they're getting closer to heaven.

SARAH   I don't...

ALAN   We've been to the moon. Sent shit out of the galaxy. See any smiting going on?

SARAH   Well.

ALAN   It's an allegory. Pure and simple. It's a way to explain languages and ambition and you know what?

SARAH   What?

ALAN   Who gives a shit! Need to believe that's true so the rest of the Bible can make an impact on your life? Who gives a damn? Need to believe… whatever! Get an imagination.

SARAH   I think it's important to remember that the point here is not…

ALAN   It's like Iraq. Need to believe Saddam's got a hand in 9/11, need to believe that he's got weapons of mass destruction trained at you in order to go in and get the job that needs doing done, so we can have a presence in the region? So that we can stop them walking around with bombs strapped to their chest. Go ahead!

SARAH   I think perhaps…

ALAN   (LOOKING AT THE PAPERS AGAIN) I've been going to church since I was a kid. Back then, in my generation. That's what we did. We went to church. Ask me if I believe in God and I'll tell you yes. Ask me if I believe in the Bible, I'll tell you yes. Ask me if this (HE HOLDS UP THE PAPER) makes any matter to me one way or the other, and I'll tell you to grow the hell up.

SARAH   It's still news.

ALAN   My mother, we're Lutherans. My mother would always say that Catholics weren't Christians. Theirs was not a faith by faith alone. These days, you know, you can't say that. We're supposed to be… tolerant.

SARAH   Yes, sir.

ALAN   My mother would say you're going to burn in hell.

SARAH   My mother would say much the same thing.

ALAN   (SMILING) Ha! Okay. Let's leave that aside for a while. What's your take on the fallout?

SARAH   I don't have one.

ALAN   What do you mean?

SARAH   I mean I don't have one. We're a news program, sir. We don't care about the fallout. We report the news, period.

ALAN   Really? How many news stories were in your overnights?

SARAH   I think…

ALAN   Twenty? Twenty-five? We get twenty-three minutes for the news. Ten for hard news. Fifteen if, you know, the president gets shot. And who decides what's in those ten?

SARAH   Sir…

ALAN   You do! I've been in the news game for fifty years sweetheart, so don't tell me we don't choose what's news and what isn't. We've been doing it for as long as there was news. So, I'll ask you again. What's the fallout?

SARAH   Two ways. It's a talking point; it vitalises the right, provides the schism with Rome that church has been looking for and turns America into a crucible of religious intolerance. Rome can't deny the cover up. But America can deny its validity.

ALAN   And the other way?

SARAH   We all become Muslims.

ALAN   One year ago I brought you in here.

SARAH   Yes, sir.

ALAN   One year ago I brought you in because it was the right thing to do.

SARAH   We're a right-wing station in an increasingly left-wing country and you wanted to put a new face on the evening news.

ALAN   You're damn right I did.

SARAH   So you brought me in and you brought Bruce in to fill the chair.

ALAN   That's right.

SARAH   A black and a Jew. Can't get more left-wing than that.

ALAN   Then you ran that damn Albania story. Over my head. Over your anchor's displeasure.

SARAH   With all respect, sir. I was doing my job.

ALAN   You went to war with the network and you lost. You lost the war, you lost the story. And you know what? I didn't give a crap.

SARAH   No, sir.

ALAN   And you know why?

SARAH   No. No, sir. I don't.

ALAN   Because everyone was talking about us. Everyone! Our logo was carried on every major network. Our shares dropped eight points overnight on that story alone, but they rose by fifteen over the next few weeks. (PAUSE) I don't give a crap about the news. I don't! I'm seventy years old and I care about one thing and one thing only. My legacy. C – N – B - C! Now, I may not have built this company but I bought it. And when I'm gone it's what will continue.

SARAH   It's news, sir. And it's wrong to hide it.

ALAN   Yes, it is. Yes, it is. So, I'm just going to ask you one more question. If you had the opportunity to go back and not run that story. Would you do it?

SARAH   No, sir. I wouldn't.

ALAN   Even though it got you moved to the mornings? That it damaged the career of everyone it touched. Even though it's gonna stop us renewing your contract?

SARAH   You're not renewing my contract because Bruce is popular with the twenty-five to forty demographics and he's asking for my ass in a sling.

ALAN   And you're giving it to him. Would – you – run – the – story!

SARAH   Yes.

ALAN   Good. 'Cos that little story lifted us into the third spot. And when I can your ass for running this one. When the network is banging down my door asking whose head is to be handed to them on a platter. You know what I'm going to say?

SARAH   John the Baptist?

ENTER DAVID.

ALAN   You've got a smart mouth on you girl. (BEAT) And I like you. (HE HANDS HER THE STORY) Put it to good use, why don't you? (TO DAVID) David.

DAVID   Alan.

EXIT ALAN.

DAVID   (CONT.) You're running it then.

SARAH   So it would seem, yes.

DAVID   He just gave you enough rope to hang yourself and you took it.

SARAH   It's… look. I don't know how many ways to say this! It's a story and we're a news program. I'm running it. Why is that so hard for you to get!

DAVID   Oh, I get it alright.

SARAH   Can we do this later? I mean. I've got a show in like, eight minutes.

DAVID PULLS A RING BOX OUT OF HIS COAT POCKET.

DAVID   I just wanted to give you this.

SARAH   Why are you wearing a coat? We're on in fifteen!

DAVID   Open the present, Sarah.

SARAH TAKES THE BOX.

SARAH   I thought you got me underwear?

DAVID   Open the box.

SHE OPENS IT TO REVEAL A SMALL, EXPENSIVE RING.

SARAH   It's beau… We're already married.

DAVID   I didn't want that to stop us.

SARAH   From what?

DAVID   Living.

SARAH   (HOLDING UP THE BAG TO HIM) I got you this.

DAVID   (TAKING IT, WARILY) What is it?

SARAH   Open it.

DAVID OPENS IT. IT'S UNDERWEAR.

DAVID   Good to see we're of one mind.

SARAH   I saw it and thought of you.

DAVID   Is that right?

SARAH	You need to get back down to hair.
DAVID	It's just what I wanted.
SARAH	You need to get back down to hair.
DAVID	You know what you could really get me?
SARAH	Don't.
DAVID	Don't run it. Not for them, not for the thing of it, for me. Us.
SARAH	Why?
DAVID	Because it'll kill you.
SARAH	It's got nothing to do with us!
DAVID	I know.
SARAH	It doesn't!
DAVID	It has to do with you.
SARAH	I just… I don't know how many fronts I can fight at the same time here.
DAVID	I know. I… I just can't watch you do this.
SARAH	Please. Just for today. Tomorrow, hell, we'll quit together. Alan pretty much made it clear…
DAVID	No. I'm sorry kid.
SARAH	You're leaving.
DAVID	Just the set for now.
SARAH	Why?
DAVID	Because I'm old. And I've done bitter. I've done bitter up to here and I don't even want to watch it anymore. (PAUSE) You know, it's snowing outside.
SARAH	Is it?
DAVID	So I guess we can't even get that right.
SARAH	This is stupid.
DAVID	I'm old. I'm entitled. Merry Christmas, sweetheart.

HE KISSES HER GENTLY ON THE CHEEK AND EXITS

STAGE RIGHT.

AL ENTERS FROM THE AUDIENCE, PAPERS IN HAND. SARAH, LOST IN THOUGHT, DOESN'T NOTICE HIM AND HE PAUSES AS HE REACHES THE STAGE.

UP TO FULL LIGHT, PIECE BY PIECE OVER 30 SECONDS. ABRUPTLY, AS IF TURNING ON A SWITCH FOR EACH INDIVIDUAL LIGHT, SPOTLIGHT ON DESK FROM FRONT.

AL   Sarah?

SARAH   (HIDING THE BOX) Al. Sorry. That the final draft?

AL   You okay?

SARAH   Fine. That's it?

AL   (HANDING HER THE PAPERS) Chris is loading it now. Was that David?

SARAH   This is good stuff, Al.

AL   Thanks.

SARAH   You write good stuff.

AL   You alright?

SARAH   This is good.

AL   Where was David going, Sarah.

SARAH   (LOOKING INTENTLY AT THE PAGES) Home. Sick.

AL   Now?

SARAH   He's been feeling lousy for days, you know how it is.

AL   Who's covering for him?

SARAH   I don't know. Bruce can handle it.

AL   Sarah... Listen, shit, I'm the last person who should be giving out marital advice...

SARAH   Yes, you are!

AL   Alright, I am but...

SARAH   What the hell were you thinking last night?

AL	Last night?
SARAH	The party!
AL	Why? What did I do?
SARAH	Why do you… How long we been working together, Al?
AL	That bad?
SARAH	I brought you in here.
AL	Listen…
SARAH	No. You listen, Al..! (PAUSE) Listen. You're right. Bruce can't handle this on his own.
AL	We'd be short.
SARAH	About two minutes.
AL	Forty.
SARAH	We'll get Josie up there with him.
CHRIS	(OFF) Producer to the control room please.
AL	The weather girl?
SARAH	And I think you should be the one to tell her.
AL	I'll need to rewrite…
SARAH	(SHAKING HER HEAD) Chris can do it. I'm heading up to the control room now.

SARAH STARTS TO EXIT UP THROUGH THE AUDIENCE.

AL	You want me to tell her she's hosting the news?
SARAH	That's right.
AL	Why?
SARAH	Because Buddhism's the only religion running for us today and I like the karma.
AL	Hey! Which one are we running with?
SARAH	Tune in and find out!

EXIT SARAH.

ENTER JOSIE.

JOSIE ENTERS STAGE LEFT, CARRYING SHEETS AS WELL. SHE IS PRACTICING HER WEATHER GIRL MOTIONS.

AL	(EXCITEDLY) Good timing.
JOSIE	(LOOKING UP) What? (NOTICING HIM) Oh.
AL	(ALL BUSINESS) Listen, I just chatted to Sarah…
JOSIE	It's too late for apologies?
AL	What?
JOSIE	I'm not interested.
AL	In hosting the news?
JOSIE	What?

AL   I just talked to Sarah. David's sick and I persuaded her to let you go on.

JOSIE	On the news?
AL	Second chair.
JOSIE	With Bruce?
AL	That a problem?
JOSIE	Sarah said this?
AL	Well, I talked to her…
JOSIE	When?
AL	Now. Ten… (LOOKS AT WATCH) Six minutes.
JOSIE	You're kidding me?

AL   (SIGNALLING OFF STAGE) Think you can handle it?

JOSIE	Sure!

ENTER NADINE.

AL   Alright. Listen. We need to get you wired for sound, alright?

JOSIE	They really want me to go on?

NADINE   (ATTACHING HER PACK) So, listen. We're just going to put this here. Like the weather, alright?

JOSIE   Thanks.

ENTER CHAD.

CHAD   Josie. Hi.

JOSIE   Chad? Right.

CHAD   Right. Chad.

JOSIE   (A LITTLE DIZZY WITH EXCITEMENT) Chad's a funny name.

CHAD   My parents are big Cincinnati fans. Sarah wanted me to give you these.

JOSIE   (TAKING THE PAPERS) What's this?

CHAD   It's the revised pages for the weather.

JOSIE   We're revising the weather?

CHAD   I think God does that.

NADINE   This goes in here. You do know it's snowing?

JOSIE   Is it?

AL   Girl doesn't miss a trick.

JOSIE   It wasn't supposed to do that!

CHAD   It'll be on the prompter. She just wanted you to familiarize yourself a little.

AL   What did you mean before.

JOSIE   Before what?

AL   Before. About the apology.

JOSIE   (SOBERING) Oh. This is because of…

AL   What?

JOSIE   Forget it.

AL   What?

JOSIE   You are such an… (SOTTO) Asshole, you know that?

AL   What did I do?

JOSIE   Last night?

AL   What?

CHAD   You gave her the Cleveland handshake.

AL   What?

JOSIE   Don't do that!

AL   Do what?

JOSIE   It's not a joke.

AL   What? What's a Cleveland handshake.

JOSIE   (ANGRY, STARTING TO UNDO THE MIC) If this is because…

CHAD   It's not.

JOSIE   How would you know?

NADINE   It's not. I was there.

AL   Could someone please tell me what the hell I'm supposed to have done!

JOSIE   You put your 'thing' in my 'hand'!

NADINE   (PAUSE) Yeah, the other thing you're going to want to know is; you're live.

CHRIS   (OFF) Can someone tell me why it's called the 'Cleveland' handshake?

AL   (TO NADINE) You were there?

CHAD   I heard it off Carol in hair.

ENTER SARAH.

EXIT NADINE.

SARAH   Josie. Can I get you at the desk, please!

AL   Come on!

JOSIE   Go fuck yourself. That live enough for you!

AL   Sarah!

SARAH   Go help Chris in the control room, Al.

AL   I never…

SARAH   Go help Chris in the control room. The vidiprinter still needs some copy, alright?

AL   Is that what she..?

SARAH   Go to the control tower or go to the door. Your choice.

AL PAUSES AND HEADS OFF, EXITING UP THROUGH THE AUDIENCE.

STAGE LEFT A MAKE UP GIRL STANDS IN THE WINGS, WAITING.

SARAH GOES OVER TO JOSIE.

CHRIS   (OFF, TANNOY) Five minutes to air.

LIGHTS DOWN ON EVERYTHING BUT THE NEWS DESK BATHED IN TV LIGHTS.

SARAH   You're going to be fine. Alright?

JOSIE   We can't just do it with one?

SARAH   We can, and that's what we're going to be doing for the most of it, but if we lose the banter we lose a little under two minutes and we don't have time to fill. Bruce will be covering the first ten, just to get you in there, but we're going to need you on the twenty.

JOSIE   The twenty?

SARAH   The second ten minutes. Fluff pieces. Don't worry. Put your ear piece in.

OVER A SPEAKER, IN AN ALMOST ELECTRONIC TONE, WE HEAR CHRIS TALKING THROUGH THE EARPIECE.

SARAH   (CONT., OFF) Can I get a sound-check?

CHRIS   (OFF, TANNOY) Josie. Hi. Can I get you to raise your right hand if you can hear me?

JOSIE RAISES HER RIGHT HAND.

SARAH   That's excellent. Listen. This is no big thing, alright? Just like the weather. Your cue cards are there. (SHE POINTS OUT

INTO THE AUDIENCE) It's Christmas so we're just using two statics.
There (SHE POINTS AGAIN) and there. (POINTING) Whichever's
got the red light on top's the one you're talking into.

JOSIE   Got it.

SARAH   Just breath through the first ten. Pick up your cues
from Bruce and have fun with it. Who knows. Do this well and they'll
be giving you your own news show.

JOSIE   Got it.

SARAH   You've got a little…

SARAH MOTIONS TO HER NOSE AND JOSIE DOES
LIKEWISE. WHEN SHE WITHDRAWS HER HAND THERE'S
BLOOD ON IT.

JOSIE   Uh oh.

SARAH   Shit.

JOSIE REACHES INTO A POCKET FOR A HANDKERCHIEF
AND PRODUCES A SMALL CHILD'S VERSION WHICH SHE
PRESSES TO HER NOSE.

JOSIE   I…

SARAH   Tilt your head back!

JOSIE   I get these sometimes, it'll pass.

SARAH HOLDS HER HEAD AND JOSIE PRESSES THE
HANKIE AGAINST HER NOSE. NADINE AND CHAD CIRCLE
THE FRONT OF THE TABLE.

SARAH   (TO MAKE UP GIRL) Tissues!

EXIT MAKE UP GIRL.

CHAD   (POINTING TO HER SHIRT) There's blood
on…

ENTER MAKE UP GIRL WITH TISSUES. SHE HANDS THEM
TO SARAH.

NADINE   Pinch the top of your nose. Run cold water over it
and stick your finger in your ear!

SARAH GLARES AT HER AND TAKES THE HANDKERCHIEF

AWAY, REPLACING IT WITH THE TISSUES.

CHAD   Blow hard.

JOSIE   It'll pass.

SARAH   (TO MAKE UP GIRL, TAKING THE TISSUES)
We're gonna need a new shirt.

EXIT MAKE UP GIRL.

SARAH   Chris, Air?

CHRIS   (OFF, TANNOY) Seven minutes.

NADINE   Take a cold pair of mettle scissors and put them on
your back. (THEY LOOK AT HER) What? It works!

JOSIE   I think I'm alright now. Really. It's stopped.

SARAH RELEASES HER HEAD. THERE DOESN'T APPEAR
TO BE BLEEDING BUT THERE IS BLOOD ON THE SHIRT.

ENTER MAKE UP GIRL WITH A NEW BLOUSE. SARAH
STEPS TENTATIVELY AWAY.

SARAH   Alright. Get changed. Chad's going to wait with
you, alright? (SHE MOTIONS TO THE MAKE UP GIRL WHO
COMES ACROSS WITH THE SHIRT) Change your shirt. You're
wired so you need something before we go on air just speak up.
Alright? But remember you're wired. Yeah?

JOSIE   Got it.

SARAH   You look fabulous.

JOSIE   Sarah?

SARAH   Yeah.

JOSIE   This doesn't. You know. I don't want this to be about
anything before…

SARAH   It's not sweetie. Honest. We'll get to that.

JOSIE   It's just that I don't think it's right.

SARAH   It's not. I promise. We'll get to it. Right now, David's
sick and we need someone on camera, okay?

JOSIE   Okay.

CHRIS   (OFF, TANNOY) Five minutes to air. Principals to stage. Quiet on set.

SARAH   I'll be right up there.

JOSIE   Okay. Thanks.

EXIT SARAH.

NADINE AND CHAD LOOK AT HER, WAITING TO SEE HER CHANGE HER SHIRT. SHE STARTS TO UNBUTTON BUT STOPS.

JOSIE   Avert your eyes.

NADINE   Avert my what?

JOSIE   Avert your eyes!

CHAD   Now who's being sexist?

JOSIE   Turn around!

NADINE   Bit young for you isn't it.

JOSIE   It's my daughter's. (THE TWO START TO TURN) (WARNING) App! (THE PAIR FACE FRONT AGAIN)

NADINE   I didn't know you had a daughter.

CHAD   I didn't know you were married?

JOSIE   I'm not. Why's it called the Cleveland handshake?

NADINE   (SHRUGGING) You've obviously never been to Cleveland?

CHAD   What's her name?

JOSIE   I'm a little busy here.

CHAD   You can tell Chad!

JOSIE   Did you just refer to yourself in the third person?

CHAD   Chad knows how to keep a secret!

JOSIE   Tell you what. You tell me the real reason why your parents called you Chad and I'll tell you what happened.

CHAD   The real reason?

JOSIE   Absolutely!

CHAD You'll think I'm lying.

JOSIE I won't. Promise.

CHAD (WITH A SHRUG) I never asked.

JOSIE You never asked?

CHAD It never came up. Why're you called Josie?

JOSIE It was my grandmother's name.

CHAD That would come up.

JOSIE You really never asked?

CHAD It didn't seem right.

JOSIE And that's the truth?

CHAD Boring, isn't it? Now…

JOSIE Sarah.

NADINE Really?

THE SHIRT CHANGE IS FINISHED. THE PAIR TURN AROUND AS JOSIE AND THE MAKE UP GIRL ADJUST THE SHIRT.

JOSIE (PAUSE. SHRUG) It's a common name.

ENTER BRUCE.

BRUCE ENTERS, HIS SHIRT COLLAR STILL PROTECTED WITH TISSUES. WIRED FOR SOUND, HIS EARPIECE IS STILL LYING ON HIS SHOULDER AS JOSIE'S WAS BEFORE.

HE STOPS SHORT WHEN HE SEES JOSIE. THE PAIR DISPERSE, LEAVING THE HANKIE ON THE TABLE, OFF CENTRE BUT CLEARLY VISIBLE.

CHAD Bruce.

EXIT CHAD AND NADINE.

BRUCE (TO THE AUDIENCE AT LARGE) Where's David?

JOSIE He's sick. (SLIGHTLY PANICKED) They didn't tell you?

BRUCE Chris?

82

CHRIS   (OFF, TANNOY) Bruce.

BRUCE   Where's David?

CHRIS   (OFF, TANNOY) He's had to go home sick. Josie's going to be covering. We'll run the ten through you using Josie as the foil then she'll pick up the first of the twenty and so on.

BRUCE   Really. Who's doing the weather? You?

JOSIE   I'm doing the weather.

CHRIS   (OFF, TANNOY) You'll pick up a double at the bottom of the twenty and we'll move her over then.

BRUCE   Okay. Sarah there.

CHRIS   (OFF, TANNOY) She's just coming in.

BRUCE   Put her on.

PAUSE.

BRUCE   (CONT.) Can you say that?

JOSIE   Ahmadinejad.

BRUCE   You'll do fine. Know who he is?

SARAH   (OFF) Bruce. David's had to go home sick.

CHRIS   (OFF, TANNOY) One minute to air. Clear the set please. Ready VTR.

EXIT MAKE UP GIRL.

BRUCE   You don't think this is something I should have been told about?

SARAH   (OFF) It just happened, Bruce. He was sick. He had to go. We needed to get Josie prepped.

BRUCE   Anything else I should know about?

SARAH   (OFF) Pick up your cues and we'll be fine.

BRUCE   You talk with Alan?

SARAH   (OFF) I did.

BRUCE   And?

SARAH   (OFF) Pick up your cues and we'll be fine.

CHRIS   (OFF, TANNOY) Thirty seconds to air. Good show, people.

BRUCE LOOKS ANGRY, THEN CHECKS HIMSELF.

BRUCE   (TO JOSIE) You'll be fine.

CHRIS   (OFF, TANNOY) Ten to air. Roll VTR. Roll sound. And five, four, three, two…

BRUCE, LOOKING DIRECTLY INTO THE AUDIENCE AS IF HE WERE LOOKING INTO A CAMERA, BEGINS TO READ THE NEWS.

CHRIS   (CONT., OFF, TANNOY) Roll tape.

BRUCE   Today. Christmas celebrations reach fever pitch in New York. (PAUSE. MUSIC INCREASE) O'Hare International closes for three hours due to ice. (PAUSE. MUSIC INCREASE) Car bomb kills three in Kinshasa amidst news of escalation. (PAUSE. MUSIC INCREASE) And we have special reports on how the weather is affecting workers and livelihoods throughout the country and how (BEAT) secret email from the Vatican might shed light on the last resting place of Jesus.

CHRIS   (OFF, TANNOY) Music up. Stand by in three, two…

BRUCE   Good morning. Christmas celebrations in New York yesterday reached an uncomfortable climax amidst the unseasonable weather. With both the famous Central Park skating rink closed and the Empire State building closing the viewing platform due to heavy rain, New Yorkers had to find other ways to entertain themselves.

CHRIS   (OFF, TANNOY) Standby tape.

BRUCE   Adrian McKinley reports.

CHRIS   (OFF, TANNOY) Roll tape.

A SIREN SOUNDS IN THE STUDIO.

CHRIS   (OFF, TANNOY) We're out. Back in one thirty.

BRUCE   (TOO LOUDLY) What the hell was that.

CHRIS   (OFF, TANNOY) What was what?

BRUCE   Get Sarah!

SARAH	(OFF) Bruce.
BRUCE	You talked to Alan?
SARAH	(OFF) I did.
BRUCE	But you're running it anyway?
SARAH	(OFF) I did and he said it was my discretion.
BRUCE	I want to speak to Alan. Get him on the phone.
SARAH	(OFF) Bruce, it's my discretion and…
BRUCE	Chris, get Alan on the phone. Now.
JOSIE	What's going on?
BRUCE	Chris, get Alan on the phone!
CHRIS	(OFF, TANNOY) There's forty-five seconds to air, Bruce.
BRUCE	Get him on the phone, I want him in the next out.
SARAH	(OFF) There's no time. The thing is up next.
BRUCE	And you're telling me about it now!
SARAH	(OFF) Decisions have to be made, Bruce, and they're my decisions to make, alright?
CHRIS	(OFF, TANNOY) Thirty seconds to live.
BRUCE	And you just expect me to read it.
SARAH	(OFF) That's what we pay you for.
BRUCE	This is why David left wasn't it? He knew what you were doing and he left?
JOSIE	What's going on?
SARAH	(OFF) David is sick, Bruce. Now sit down and do your damn job, alright?
CHRIS	(OFF, TANNOY) Ten to live.

BRUCE THINKS FOR A SECOND.

CHRIS	(CONT., OFF, TANNOY) And five, four, three…
BRUCE	Reports continue to come in, however, of above normal church…

CHRIS   (OFF, TANNOY, OVERLAP) Um Bruce, that's not on your script.

BRUCE   … attendance at the midnight Mass, which is a good thing. Josie. Your parents are from New York. Any Christmas cheer?

JOSIE   Umm. I tell you, Bruce. It's just another normal Christmas for them. Whatever the weather.

BRUCE   Will they be attending Mass?

SARAH   (OFF) Bruce, cut it out!

JOSIE   Well, I tell you, Bruce. They're Mormon so… they probably won't.

BRUCE LOOKS A LITTLE SURPRISED BY THIS BUT RECOVERS HIS COMPOSURE FAST.

SARAH   (OFF) Good answer Josie.

BRUCE   Well, a happy holiday to everyone in New York.

SARAH   (OFF) Let's just get through this shall we.

BRUCE   In other news. The religious… (HE PAUSES) I'm sorry. (HE MOVES TO A PIECE OF PAPER ON HIS DESK) Reports out of O'Hare…

CHRIS   (OFF, TANNOY) Bruce?

BRUCE   …today were sketchy as to why a tank full of…

SARAH   (OFF, OVERLAP) You little bastard! Read what's on the card!

BRUCE   …water was accidentally spilled over a main runway, stranding…

CHRIS   (OFF, TANNOY, OVERLAP) I need time for the VTR! Someone get the goddamned tape of O'Hare cued up.

BRUCE   …hundreds of holiday passengers eager to get home for the holidays as the ice froze over, leaving a Central Park-like skating rink which literally…

SARAH   (OFF, EAR, OVERLAP) You little bastard. Josie, (JOSIE LOOKS UP) don't react. We need time for the tape so just follow my lead. Bruce. Segue. Now!

BRUCE   …'froze' the airport for nearly three hours as crews struggled to clean up. Luckily no-one was hurt. Our Chris Stern has the report but before we go to him; Josie. How important is it that our airports stay open at Christmas?

SARAH   (OFF, EAR, OVERLAP) It's very important, Bruce.

JOSIE   (COPYING) I'm… It's very important, Bruce.

SARAH   (OFF, EAR, OVERLAP) Over five million people travel home over the holidays and the airports are our lifeblood for that.

JOSIE   (COPYING) Over five million people travel home over the holidays and the airports are our lifeblood for that.

BRUCE   Are you flying home this year?

SARAH   (OFF, EAR, OVERLAP) Whatever you want. (QUICKLY) Don't say that just…

JOSIE   I'll be on the first plane out after the show.

SARAH   (OFF, EAR) Good girl.

CHRIS   (OFF, TANNOY) VTR in five…

BRUCE   Well we wish you a happy trip. Here's Bruce… Sorry, here's Chris Stern with the report.

SARAH   (OFF, EAR) I'm coming down.

CHRIS   (OFF, TANNOY) And we're out. Ninety to live. I'm gonna wanna know what to run here?

JOSIE   Wow!

BRUCE   You did great.

ENTER SARAH.

SARAH ENTERS FROM THE AUDIENCE, CROSSING QUICKLY. SHE'S SHOUTING BEFORE SHE'S EVER GOT TO THE FLOOR.

SARAH   You read the cards that I give you!

BRUCE   (OVERLAP) That was completely unprofessional.

SARAH   Unprofessional! You read the damn cards.

BRUCE   I'm not doing it. I'm sorry, but…

SARAH   You're a mouth jockey!

BRUCE   I'm sorry?

SARAH   A mouth jockey. You say the words, you don't get to make up content!

BRUCE   My contract…

SARAH   You read the goddamn words, I goddamn give you. You're lucky I don't fire you on the spot!

BRUCE   My contract…

SARAH   I don't care what your damn contract says. You read the words!

BRUCE   You blindsided me.

SARAH   I what?

BRUCE   You blindsided me and you know it! That's why you had David leave.

SARAH   David's sick.

BRUCE   Bullshit!

CHRIS   (OFF, TANNOY) Thirty to air. I need to know what we're running here, people.

SARAH   (INTO HER MOUTH PIECE) We're running it.

BRUCE   No! We move on!

SARAH   What? You'll read what I goddamned give you or…

CHRIS   (OFF, TANNOY) Bruce is right. I need time for the tape. We need to run something else.

SARAH   What's up next?

CHRIS   (OFF, TANNOY) The weather thing.

SARAH   How long's VTR?

CHRIS   (OFF, TANNOY) Sixty.

SARAH   Chris. Standby to run the thing after that. (TO BRUCE) Segue. Quickly!

CHRIS   (OFF, TANNOY) Ten to live.

BRUCE   (REINSERTING HIS EARPIECE) I'm not reading it.

SARAH   You damn well are!

CHRIS   (OFF, TANNOY) Live in five, four, three, two…

SARAH STEPS BACK OUT OF CAMERA SHOT BUT REMAINS ON THE STUDIO FLOOR, GABBING THE HANKIE OFF THE TABLE AS SHE DOES SO.

BRUCE   Thank you, um, Chris. I think I speak for everyone here at CNB when I wish everyone out there a safe journey this Christmas. (PAUSE) But the weather isn't only affecting travel this Christmas. The unseasonable climate has affected ski areas and winter holiday resorts throughout the country.

CHRIS   (OFF, TANNOY) Five seconds to VTR

BRUCE   Mike Mitchell reports.

THE BUZZER SOUNDS.

CHRIS   (OFF, TANNOY) And we're out. Sixty to live. Sarah. What's the plan?

SARAH   (OVERLAP, STEPPING FORWARD AGAIN) Now, you listen to me…

BRUCE   I will not read that. It's wrong.

SARAH   You will read what I put in front of you or you're out of here!

BRUCE   Really. And how are you going to explain that to corporate? I don't care what you say, I'm not reading…

SARAH   (TURNING TO JOSIE) Josie. As soon as we go live, I want you to…

JOSIE   I can't read that.

SARAH   It's news!

JOSIE   I can't do it. I mean, it's too much. My first time!

BRUCE   You can't ask her to…

SARAH   Stay out of this, Bruce.

CHRIS   (OFF, TANNOY) Thirty to live. Sarah?

JOSIE   You can't ask me to read this.

SARAH   Most people would give their... Look, you want to read the news or you want to read the news?

JOSIE   I am reading the news! But you can't...

SARAH   (ANGRILY) Shit! Chris, run Kinshasa and go straight to break after. (SHE POINTS AT BRUCE) As soon as we're off the air, we talk.

BRUCE   As soon as we're off the air, I'm on the phone to
Alan.

CHRIS   (OFF, TANNOY) Ten to live.

SARAH   Get your lawyer while you're at it! Because we will sue your ass back to local broadcasting!

CHRIS   (OFF, TANNOY) Five, four, three, two...

SARAH   (OVERLAP) You're a fucking mouthpiece!

BLACKOUT.

END OF SCENE.

SCENE 2

BACKSTAGE.

LIGHTS UP ON A BACKSTAGE AREA, FILLED WITH WIRES AND CABLES. HALF LIGHT, SINGLE SPOT COMING FROM STAGE LEFT ILLUMINATING THE STAGE. STAGE RIGHT DARK.

SARAH STANDS CENTRE STAGE, A LIGHT STAGE LEFT WHERE THE NEWS DESK IS, BATHES HER.

CHRIS   (OFF, TANNOY) We're out. Seven minutes to air.

SARAH   Chris?

CHRIS   (OFF, TANNOY) Go.

SARAH   What have we got in the twenty?

CHRIS   (OFF, TANNOY) Um. Homeless Santa. >>*WGA*<<, Bethlehem and Taylor Swift.

SARAH   Okay. This is what we're going to do. Josie, I'll need you to talk her through this, Josie'll run the homeless Santa, then Bruce, then Josie. Tell Al we're going to need a segue, then we end with the thing. 'Special report' blah blah blah.

CHRIS   (OFF, TANNOY) Listen, Sarah. I'm with you on this, alright, but maybe it's time we passed this off. I can speak to Gareth…

SARAH   We're running the story, Chris.

CHRIS   (OFF, TANNOY) And if he won't?

SARAH   (TO CHRIS) He will.

CHRIS   (OFF, TANNOY) And if he won't?

ENTER BRUCE.

SARAH   (TO CHRIS) I'm talking to him now. (TO BRUCE) Turn it off.

BRUCE   Listen…

SARAH   You're hot. I am not having this conversation with everyone. Turn it off!

BRUCE REACHES AROUND AND TURNS HIS MIC OFF AT THE BOX.

BRUCE   Listen!

SARAH   (ANGRILY) You read the words I goddamned give you!

BRUCE   Or what? The way I see it you're done at this network, so give me one good reason I should do anything you say.

SARAH   It's news!

BRUCE   It's not news! Stop saying that. News is when children can't get education. News is a fire that kills eight homeless people in a supposedly empty apartment. News is economy, business, politics, overseas events and yes, news might even be a president getting a blow job off an intern but this; this is not news. This is belief!

SARAH   It's not news that the largest religion in the Western hemisphere might just have been hiding a salient fucking fact about it for the last two thousand years?

BRUCE   No! It's not! Look, people's belief has nothing, nothing to do with facts whatsoever, it doesn't! Was there an ark, was there not an ark? Was Jesus married? Did he actually walk on water or windsurf! None of this matters. It's what it is to them, what it means to them that matters, not whether or not somebody could or could not be Jesus.

SARAH   They lied about it!

BRUCE   And they should be hung out to dry for it! But not here. Not by us! We put that out on the air and we're no better than the Taliban! Religion, people's faith, has absolutely nothing to do with us and it shouldn't be part of what we do, period! And I think this is less about any desire to 'tell the news' than it is about you and you know it.

SARAH   What's that supposed to mean?

BRUCE   It means three months ago you ran a story that was anti-American…

SARAH   It was not!

BRUCE   It was anti-American and it was anti this network. I disagreed with you, shit I think even David disagreed with you, but you ran it anyway! And it got both of us moved to the morning news.

SARAH   And you've spent the last three months kissing up to corporate for it.

BRUCE   Yes, I have. Yes I damn well have. Because I like my job, Sarah. I like what I do.

SARAH   They brought you in here because of your skin!

BRUCE   So what? Of course they brought me in because of my skin! But they keep me because I'm good!

SARAH   They keep you because you're a pussy!

BRUCE   Fuck you! In three months time I'll be back on the nine and you'll be back doing infomercials for PBS. Excuse me if I don't want you to take me with you because you think you have a higher sense of journalistic value that me.

SARAH   I do have a higher sense of journalistic value than you. And you know what? All your Taliban bullshit. I don't believe a fucking word of it! You're not doing this because you think it's not news, you're doing this because I got you bumped to the morning!

BRUCE   You're goddamned right I am! That was my slot. Mine! I disagreed with you and I was right.

SARAH   You were not right! You weren't. News is news. We don't get to say what it is, we report it! We were the face of liberalism on his network. That's what they brought us in here for! But there's no point being a face of something if you're not the real thing behind it.

BRUCE   You're calling me a liar?

SARAH   Yes, I'm calling you a liar.

BRUCE   Say what you damn well like but you say anything like that in public and I will have your ass so full of lawyers you'll have to shit out of your ears.

BRUCE TURNS TO GO.

SARAH   I know about the marriage.

BRUCE STOPS.

BRUCE   What marriage?

SARAH   I know that you did it in England, maybe because it's legal, maybe so you didn't have to register it back here or maybe because no one there knows who the hell you are.

BRUCE   Wow. You must really hate me.

SARAH   God, Bruce. It wasn't enough you were ethnic. You had to be gay as well!

BRUCE   You fucking hypocrite!

SARAH   You want to…

BRUCE   This is why I hate the term liberal. I didn't even vote last time! There's a man out there who last night put his penis into the hand of one of your staff and you've yet to raise a word about it but I'm gay and you're straight in with the attack dogs.

SARAH   What can I say? It's news. You said it yourself. A president gets a blow job off an intern or the black presenter of a conservative network hides his sexuality by getting married in another country? News!

BRUCE   It's personal.

SARAH   Is it? You're a member of the NAACP, why not gay pride as well? Is it that you thought it might be one minority too many for a career such as ours? (PAUSE) Did you really think no one was going to find out?

BRUCE   It's no one else's business.

SARAH   God, Bruce. I can't tell whether you're naive or just plain stupid.

CHRIS   (OFF, TANNOY) Two minutes to live.

BRUCE   Dammit. So this is what it is, is it? This is a shakedown.

SARAH   This is what it is.

BRUCE   I don't read it and you go to corporate, that it?

SARAH   You just refused to read a news item on air. You think that's not going to get out? Christmas morning be damned!

BRUCE   And you think that's going to go bad with me on this network? You know Alan's just letting you run it so they can fire you. You do know that?

SARAH   This is news, Bruce. I'm not asking that you agree with it. I'm just asking you to do your job. That's all.

BRUCE SEEMS TO BE THINKING ABOUT IT.

SARAH   (CONT.) Look. What you do… I don't care about the marriage thing. I really don't. I don't give a shit whether you like men, women or poultry. You're good at your job. But I'm good at mine. They brought me in here to do a job and when I didn't they bumped me and you know what, so what? It doesn't matter! When it happened I had the support of absolutely no one in the news room. Not David, not Chris and most importantly, not you. We were a team Bruce. A team!

BRUCE   David stood by you.

SARAH   No he didn't. To my face he did, but he was glad when they moved me here with him. They moved me to a morning show with a misogynist writer and nubile weather girl. You know what that does to a career like mine? But you! You were supposed to be on my side!

BRUCE   It's Christmas, Sarah.

SARAH   We're a news program, Bruce. We don't do holidays.

CHRIS   (OFF, TANNOY) One minute to air. Principals to the stage please.

THEY LOOK AT EACH OTHER.

BRUCE   It was David, wasn't it? The thing.

SARAH   It doesn't matter.

BRUCE   I said something to him… We were in a bar and I said that marriage laws in the UK…

SARAH   It doesn't matter.

BRUCE   No newsman like an old newsman, right?

SARAH   Do your job and we won't have a problem.

BRUCE   Tell me, Sarah. Did David leave you because he didn't agree with the story or because he couldn't stand seeing you like this?

SARAH   David didn't leave me. He left the show.

BRUCE   And you're sure there's a difference.

CHRIS   (OFF, TANNOY) Thirty seconds to air. Bruce? I need you in your seat.

SARAH   Just… Do your job, alright?

BRUCE   (TURNING TO GO AND STOPPING) I always do my job but, and there's really no way of getting around this; you had two news stories could have canned tonight and you chose to drop the one about a five year old rape victim.

EXIT BRUCE.

CHRIS   (OFF, TANNOY) Thirty seconds to air.

SARAH STANDS IN THE MIDDLE OF THE ROOM, LOOKING TIRED. SHE REACHES AROUND AND PLUGS HER MIC BACK IN.

CHRIS   (CONT., OFF, EAR) Sarah?

SARAH   Run the story.

CHRIS   (OFF, EAR) He'll do it?

SARAH   Run the story, Chris.

SHE STANDS, DEFLATED IN THE MIDDLE OF THE ROOM, THEN MOVES SLOWLY TOWARDS THE ENTRANCE TO THE STAGE, WATCHING WHAT'S GOING ON.

CHRIS   (OFF, MIC) Cue music. (THE SAME THEME MUSIC AS AT THE BEGINNING STARTS PLAYING) We're live in five, four, three, two…

SARAH STANDS AT THE DOOR.

BRUCE   (OFF) Welcome back. This is CNB News. I'm Bruce Baxter.

JOSIE   And I'm Josie Lawrence. (PAUSE) The true meaning of Christmas often gets forgotten amidst the fun and festivities but for one 'Santa' this year, it came through loud and clear. Bob Ealing. A fifty-four year old sheet metal worker in Richmond Virginia has played Santa for the last fifteen years at the local mall. This year however, Bob was evicted from his home due to non-payment of tax following his wife's death and found himself homeless, only a week into the season. Trevor Nugent has the report.

THE BUZZER SOUNDS.

CHRIS   (OFF, TANNOY) We're out. One forty to live.

TREVOR   (V/O) When the parishioners at Saint Martin's saw Santa sleeping in a manger they thought it was some new-aged ploy to drum up attendance. But for Bob Ealing, it was anything but a stunt. Father Kyle Harrond, a priest at Saint Martin's for nearly thirty years had this to say.

PRIEST   (V/O) I think the problem is that, for the last ten years or so, we've had to lock the door because of vandals. Everyone here knows Bob. He's been in the flock since he was a child. I guess he thought the doors would be open.

TREVOR   (V/O) What was the reaction when they found Santa, rather than Jesus in the manger?

PRIEST   (V/O) We had a kids party for members of the choir that morning, you know, when they saw Santa they started going up to him, wanting to talk.

TREVOR   (V/O) And you've kept him here ever since.

PRIEST   (V/O) One of the things we've forgotten about Christmas in the battle against secularism, is that the whole idea of giving presents is to show your love of the people around you. And what's more Christian than that? If Christ was here today, he'd be the first person giving everything he's got.

TREVOR   (V/O) Secular or not, Bob has proved a big hit and Father Harrond is expecting a huge crowd for midnight Mass.

PRIEST   (V/O) We're going to have him giving presents at the doorway. He's a big hit. Who knows, maybe at Easter we'll crucify him.

BRUCE   (OFF, LAUGHING) Something to look forward to, I suppose. (BEAT) Speaking of bright horizons >>*it seems the writers' strike may soon be over, with several prominent shows promising to return in the New Year.*<< Sandy Thomas has the inside line.

SANDY   >>*US talk show star Jon Stewart has said production will resume on his award-winning Daily next month, despite the continued Hollywood writers' strike.*<<

SARAH   (INTO HER EAR) Chris?

CHRIS   (OFF, EAR) Sarah?

SARAH   Pull it.

CHRIS   (OFF, EAR) You're sure?

SARAH   Pull it. Run the rest of the twenty.

CHRIS   (OFF, EAR) Yeah.

SARAH   Call Gareth and tell him to expect a call later today. From one of the papers. Tell him… tell him it's not news. Not today at least, and he should sell it.

CHRIS   (OFF, EAR) Okay.

SANDY   >>*The show will return with new episodes on 7 January, but without its writing staff who have been on strike since November 5th.*

The Daily Show's spin-off series, The Colbert Report, will also resume on 7 January, with both shows airing on the Comedy Central TV network.

However, as both Stewart and Colbert are members of the Writers Guild of America (WGA), they are barred from penning any new material - even for themselves.

In a joint statement, the hosts said: "We would like to return to work with our writers. If we cannot, we would like to express our ambivalence, but without our writers we are unable to express something as nuanced as ambivalence."

The WGA reacted angrily to the announcement, saying: "Comedy Central forcing Jon Stewart and Stephen Colbert back on the air will not give the viewers the quality shows they've come to expect."

The union also announced this week, however, it would refuse to grant a special waiver to allow producers of the Oscars and the Golden Globes to hire union writers for their shows. Though promoters are hopeful of reversing that decision soon.<<

SARAH   (INTO THE PHONE) Yeah. You're watching? (PAUSE) No. (PAUSE) Who do you know over at the New York Times? (PAUSE) Yeah. (PAUSE) No. I'll… I'll come straight home. (PAUSE) Yeah. Yeah. (PAUSE) You do that. (PAUSE) I miss you too. (PAUSE) David? (BEAT) Merry Christmas.

BRUCE   And finally. The ch…(PAUSE) I'm sorry. In other news, troubled pop star Taylor Swift is in the news again after spending the night with one of the paparazzi tailing her, only days after failing to appear in court citing exhaustion. Jason Knott has this report.

CHRIS   (OFF, TANNOY) We're out. Ninety seconds to live.

BLACKOUT.

END OF ACT III.

CURTAINS.

Artwork & Photos from original production

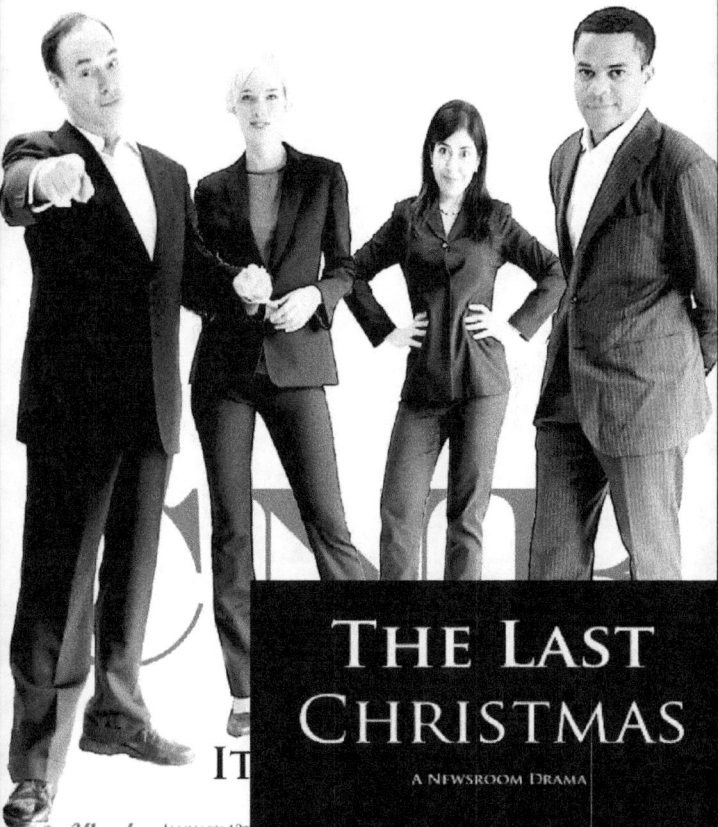

A BRAND NEW PLAY BY ALEC HARRIS

THE LAST CHRISTMAS

Woody
Theatre

JANUARY 12T
JANUARY 13T
JANUARY 14T

www.newworlds

A NEW

IT

THE LAST
CHRISTMAS

A NEWSROOM DRAMA

Also by

DIRECT
LIGHT

<small>Thomas Alexander</small>

THOMAS ALEXANDER

THE VISITOR

BY

THOMAS ALEXANDER

THE VISITOR

WHEN THE LOVER OF A FAMOUS
WRITER GOES MISSING IN A WAR
RAVAGED COUNTRY, HE BRIBES HIS
WAY INTO A JAIL TO QUESTION
HER HUSBAND, A MISSIONARY,
WHO IS BEING TORTURED AS A
TRAINING EXERCISE BY HIS CAPTORS.

ALONE IN THE CELL, THE TWO
START A DIALOGUE ABOUT THE
NATURE OF BELIEF.

BELIEF IN GOD, LOVE AND POLITICS.

MURDER ME GENTLY

By

THOMAS ALEXANDER

"ONE MAN... ONE WOMAN... AND THE QUEST FOR JUSTICE IN AN UNJUST WORLD"

MODERN DAY RUSSIA THROUGH THE MEDIUM OF FILM NOIR

BLENDING REAL LIFE EVENTS WITH COMEDY AND INTRIGUE, *MURDER ME GENTLY'S* UNIQUE PERSPECTIVE ON THE WORLD OF RUSSIAN POLITICS AS SEEN THROUGH THE LENS OF FILM NOIR, SPANS THE ASSASINATION OF INTERNATIONALLY RENOWNED JOURNALISTS, PUTIN'S REACH FOR THE RETURN OF SOVIET SATELITE STATES, AND THE INFLITRATION OF GOVERNMENT BY OLIGARCHS AND CRIMINALS.

PROVIDING A DAMNING INDICTMENT OF THE WEST'S INABILITY TO HALT MOSCOW'S POLICY OF EXPANSIONISM *MURDER ME GENTLY* LENDS A THEATRICAL EXPOSE TO THE VERY REAL WORLD OF CORRUPTION AND GREED IN INTERNATIONAL POLITICS TODAY.

A CONMAN, A DISGRACED INTERPOL AGENT, A MAFIA BOSS, A CIA SPOOK, AND THE SECRET TO THE FUTURE ALL UNITE IN AN UNLIKELY ALLIANCE IN A LOVE AFFAIR THAT WILL DEFINE THE FATE OF THE WORLD IN THOMAS ALEXANDER'S

... MURDER ME ... GENTLY!

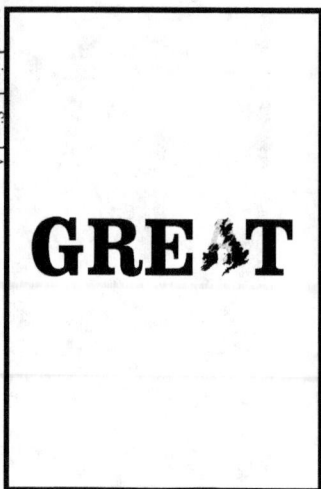

GREAT

GREAT

BY

THOMAS ALEXANDER

A REMOTE ROOM IN THE THROES OF WINTER.

THE ONCE GREAT MAN LIVES ALONE NOW WITH HIS SON,

AN OLD FRIEND HAS COME TO VISIT. HE HAS CLIMBED UP FROM THE VILLAGE IN ORDER TO OFFER THE OLD MAN ONE LAST CHANCE TO ESCAPE THE ENCROACHING WINTER THAT IS ABOUT TO TAKE HIM, STIRRING UP MEMORIES OF BETTER TIMES AND THE WARMTH OF SUMMER.

BEGAT

By

THOMAS ALEXANDER

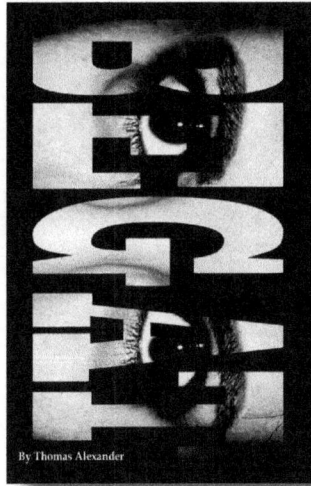

By Thomas Alexander

IN A COUNTRY, AFTER THE WAR, A JUDGE THROWS A DINNER PARTY, SEEKING SUPPORT AGAINST A POWERFUL MINISTER WHO HAS RAPED AND KILLED A SERVANT GIRL.

BUT THE JUDGE HIMSELF IS THE TARGET TONIGHT, AND THE SHADOW OF THE WAR HE SO DESPERATELY WANTS TO LEAVE BEHIND THREATENS TO ENGULF HIS FAMILY AS A YOUNG WOMAN SEEKS REVENGE FOR THE SINS OF HIS PAST.

A BREA
Happiness

NOT EVERY DOOR SHOULD BE OPENED.

HAPPINESS

BY

THOMAS ALEXANDER

ON A REMOTE HEADLAND IN NORTH WALES A MAN AND HIS PARAPLEGIC SON DREAM OF LIFE BEYOND THE CONFINES OF THEIR FOUR WALLS.

BUT WHEN A WOMAN OFFERS THEM THE ESCAPE THEY SO CRAVE THEY FIND THEY ARE BOUND BY MORE THAN THEIR DREAMS.

THE JEALOUSY OF A BORED POLICEMAN AND THE KINDNESS OF A MAIL ORDER BRIDE SET THEM ON A PATH OF HOPE AND DESTRUCTION.

THE LAST CHRISTMAS

BY

THOMAS ALEXANDER

WHEN AN EMBATTLED NEWSROOM RECEIVES A POTENTIALLY EARTH SHATTERING STORY MINUTES BEFORE AIR ON CHRISTMAS DAY THE CAREFUL EQUILIBRIUM OF THE TEAM IS SHATTERED AND OLD DIVIDING LINES COME TO THE FORE, TURNING CO-WORKER AGAINST CO-WORKER.

SET IN REAL TIME AND INCORPORATING ACTUAL AND INTERCHANGEABLE NEWS EVENTS THE LAST CHRISTMAS PITS SOCIAL POLITICS AGAINST JOURNALISTIC INTEGRITY IN A BATTLE OF THE ETHICS.

GOD

By

Thomas Alexander

When the named partner of a small law firm dies, leaving large debt, the remaining misfits of the firm are forced to take on just about any client available, including a litigious soccer-mom who would like to sue God for the death of her husband, hit by a lightning bolt on the 15th hole of a municipal golf course.

The Trial becomes complicated however, when an indigent with no background and a canny knack of knowing everyone's background enters the courtroom claiming to be 'God'.

Batting back and fore between the courtroom and the personal lives of the lawyers, God is a fast paced courtroom drama/comedy that uses original staging and non-linear storytelling to provide a lighthearted, but complex social drama.

THE FAMILY

BY

THOMAS ALEXANDER

TODAY, FOR THE FIRST TIME IN LONGER THAN ANYONE CAN REMEMBER, THE FAMILY ARE GATHERING. THEY ARE GATHERING TO CELEBRATE THE ENGAGEMENT OF THE MATERNAL NIECE, THEY ARE GATHERING TO CELEBRATE THE LAST BIRTHDAY OF THE PATRIARCH, THEY ARE GATHERING TO WELCOME HOME THE PRODIGAL SON AND HIS BEAUTIFUL GIRLFRIEND, AND THEY ARE GOING TO CELEBRATE ALL THIS WITH A SLIDESHOW.

CANDID PHOTOGRAPHS. PHOTOGRAPHS OF THINGS NO ONE THOUGHT ANYONE ELSE KNEW ABOUT. PHOTOGRAPH TAKEN WHEN NO ONE ELSE WAS THERE.

IT'S ALL COMING OUT TODAY. IN BLACK AND WHITE FOR EVERYONE TO SEE. THE REMNANTS OF CHILD ABUSE, INFIDELITY, LOSS, DESTRUCTION, AND MISSED BIRTHDAY PARTIES. IT'S ALL COMING OUT. IT'S GOING TO BE A LONG NIGHT. POSSIBLY FOREVER.

The Recruitment Officer

By

Thomas Alexander

Tom, a charming Yankee recruiter, comes to an unspecified English town and falls in love with the conference centre manager, Julia.

But what exactly is he recruiting for? Why does everyone who joins never come back and what is on the other side of the door

Where do the recruits go after signing up?

An existential love story that asks questions of who we are, what we want from life and whether we're getting it, The Recruitment Officer is a remodelling of the 1706 play by George Farquhar, *The Recruiting Officer*.

Writer's Block

By

Thomas Alexander

Paul Block was once a prolific writer. A recipient of both the Pen and Faulkner awards and the author of over ten different novels, he was once considered the UK's most up and coming writer until, at the age of forty, he suffered a nervous breakdown.

Ten years later the world has forgotten Paul Block. Holed up in his study he has been working on the same first page of his new novel for nearly five years, kept company by only his maid, a foul mouthed Irish hit-man, a veteran of the battle of Gettysburg, and a nineteen forties femme fatale.

Today, all that's going to change. Paul has a busy day ahead of him. First he's going to kill a persistent and charmless young reporter who wants to do a piece on 'writer's block' and then he's going to have a rare visit from his son who's bringing him bad news and a new couch.

With a missing body and a son who hates him, Paul must finally rid himself of his protagonists if he's ever going to stay out of jail, and finish that first page.

THOMAS

Japan, 1945 – A Family At War

When a wandering priest escaping a troubled past is taken in by a prominent family, a quiet city in northern Japan is forced to confront the dark shadows of war seeping into their lives in ways they could never have anticipated.

With its townsmen scattered throughout the farthest ends of a desperate empire in a final defence against the encroaching West, the idyllic northern city of Morioka, far removed from the harsh realities of the front, is largely left to itself.

THOMAS ALEXANDER

But when a prominent doctor is conscripted and sent to Manila, his sister is left as head of the household and must deal with a young priest living at the bottom of their garden with a large collection of maps and strange knowledge of English.

A Scattering of Orphans

As the cold hand of war approaches, each person must choose their own destiny and place in the new world.

THE OTHER SIDE

ALEXANDER

Commemorating the 70th Anniversary of the end of WW2! A trilogy spanning the length of the war from the viewpoint of an ordinary Japanese family.

Thomas Alexander

The Disingenuous Martyr

omas Alexander

Beyond The Noonday Sun

Offering a unique perspective through the eyes of a rural Japanese family into the impact of history's bloodiest war to date, *A Scattering of Orphans* is one family's attempt to make sense of a changing world amidst the desolation of war, both home and abroad.

DIRECT LIGHT

OF THE SUN